Y0-CQE-362

PSYCHOSOCIAL NEEDS OF THE AGED:

A Health Care Perspective

REVISED

Edited by Eugene Seymour

This monograph is published by the
Ethel Percy Andrus Gerontology Center
University of Southern California

Richard H. Davis, Ph. D.
Director of Publications and Media Projects

THE UNIVERSITY OF SOUTHERN CALIFORNIA PRESS

ISBN 0-88474-048-x

Library of Congress Catalog Card Number 78-60818

Managing Editor: Richard Bohen
Editorial Assistant: Jean Rarig

Authors

Vern L. Bengtson, Ph.D., Professor of Sociology, University of Southern California, Los Angeles, California

Esther Lucile Brown, Ph.D., Consultant on Psychological Aspects of Patient Care and Trends in Health Service, San Francisco, California

Irene Mortenson Burnside, R.N., M.S., Author/Lecturer, Monte Sereno, California

Louis Gelwicks, A.I.A., President, Gerontological Planning Associates, 2800 Neilson Way, Santa Monica, California

Elsie A. Giorgi, M.D., Associate Clinical Professor of Medicine, School of Medicine, University of California at Los Angeles; Private practice in Internal Medicine, Beverly Hills, California

Elsbeth Kahn, Ph.D., Associate Professor, Department of Community and Family Medicine, School of Medicine, University of Southern California, Los Angeles, California.

Lois N. Knowles, R.N., Ph.D., Professor of Nursing and formerly Assistant Dean, College of Nursing, University of Florida, Gainesville, Florida

Maxine Patrick, R.N., Dr.P.H., Professor, Department of Physiological Nursing, University of Washington School of Nursing, Seattle, Washington

Gordon Purdy, M.S.W., Director, Senior Health Improvement Programs, Handmaker Jewish Geriatric Center, Tucson, Arizona.

Valerie L. Remnet, R.H., M.S.W., L.C.S.W., Mental Health Project Director, Andrus Gerontology Center, University of Southern California, Los Angeles; Lecturer, Department of Nursing, California State University at Long Beach, California

Arthur N. Schwartz, Ph.D., Clinical Psychologist and Staff Associate for Long Term Care, Andrus Gerontology Center, University of Southern California, Los Angeles, California

Eugene Seymour, M.D., M.P.H., Medical Director, Wilshire Center Geriatrics Medical Group; Adjunct Associate Professor, Andrus Gerontology Center, University of Southern California, Los Angeles, California

Alexander Simon, M.D., Professor of Psychiatry Emeritus, School of Medicine, University of California at San Francisco, California

Ruth B. Weg, Ph.D., Associate Professor of Biology and Gerontology, Andrus Gerontology Center, University of Southern California, Los Angeles, California.

Introduction

In 1973 the Andrus Gerontology Center published *The Psychosocial Needs of the Aged: Selected Papers,* information which had been presented to nurses at a series of workshops at the Center. Those workshops, held in the early 70's, had been designed to answer requests from nurses themselves for information in this special area. A continuing demand for the publication has indicated that a substantial need for such knowledge still exists.

This 1978 version of the original publication, retitled *The Psychosocial Needs of the Aged: A Health View Perspective,* has been expanded for use of nurses and others working with older persons. The new chapters address both clinical and psychosocial needs of this group.

The chapter on health assessment leads the professional nurse from the role of passive purveyor of medication to the more active role of collector of physiologic data, interpreter of that data, and initiator of health service based on that information. It is hoped that this exploratory chapter will stimulate its readers to further study of manifestations of diseases in the elderly.

The discussion of psychosocial needs of elderly in the community expands on a preceding chapter and gives specific recommendations for solutions. The new chapter on day health care describes an increasingly-evident phenomenon: development of alternatives to the institutionalization of the homebound, frail, and disabled elderly. The final section, a training program for staff, should be a practical tool for the helping professions.

Sincere appreciation is expressed to those authors who cooperated in the publication of the original edition as well as to those contributors whose new chapters have expanded the usefulness of this monograph.

Eugene Seymour, M.D.

Contents

INTRODUCTION   v

ASSESSMENT

  1. Health Assessment of the Elderly
      Eugene Seymour   1

CHANGES

  2. Physiological Changes that Influence Patient Care
      Ruth B. Weg   7

  3. Psychological Changes That Influence Patient Care
      Alexander Simon   19

NEEDS

  4. Needs, Environmental Design, and Health Care of
      the Aged
      Louis Gelwicks   29

  5. The Institutionalized Aged and Their Social Needs
      Vern L. Bengtson   35

  6. Psychosocial Needs of the Aged in General Hospitals
      Maxine Patrick   39

  7. Psychosocial Needs of the Aged in Nursing Homes
      Elsbeth Kahn   43

  8. Psychosocial Needs of the Aged: What Nurses
      Can Do
      Esther Lucile Brown   46

  9. Psychosocial Needs of Older Adults in the
      Community
      Valerie L. Remnet   54

CARE

 10. Nursing and the Psychosocial Care of the
      Institutionalized Aged
      Irene Mortenson Burnside   63

 11. Utilizing the Health Team in the Care of the Aged
      Elsie A. Giorgi   72

 12. Standards for Geriatric Nursing Care: The Where,
      Who, How, Why, What, and When of It
      Lois N. Knowles   80

13. The Adult Day Care Center Experience
(SHIP, Tucson, Arizona)
Gordon Purdy   96

STAFF TRAINING

14. A Training Program for Psychosocial Dimensions
of Care in Long Term Care Facilities
Arthur N. Schwartz   102

Health Assessment of the Elderly

1

Eugene Seymour, M.D., M.P.H.

The field of health assessment has long been the purview of the physician, though recently the need for assessment has expanded to such a degree that new groups of health professionals are being trained in this art. Thus, physicians and nurses with extensive clinical experience could well skip this chapter, since it is written primarily for those new to clinical geriatrics as well as for those whose clinical skills may be somewhat rusty. The concept of "health assessment" is a significant departure from previous concepts of patient evaluation. The medical aspects become only one area to assess, with social, psychological, and environmental factors demanding equal attention. This concept places the observer in an important and rather pivotal position, in that accurate information must be collected, screened, interpreted, and then passed on for disposition.

This chapter will concentrate on health assessment in emergency and semi-emergency situations. Overall health assessment of the elderly, including details of organ-by-organ evaluation in depth, will be discussed in a forthcoming book. Some of the cardinal rules (the list is incomplete; please make your own additions) are as follows:

1. Don't be afraid of talking to or examining an older patient
2. Sophisticate your ability to take and record the vital signs
3. Learn to assess the degree of urgency which exists in a supposed emergency situation
4. Learn to report as accurately and concisely as possible your findings to the physician
5. Practice, practice, practice

Most people, when faced with an emergency situation, often panic; and they temporarily lose their observational skills and cease to be of significant value to the patient in the moment of need. Most health professionals are trained to take orders in emergency situations; only a few are able to give orders and also activate additional procedures based on their observations. Parenthetically, it is of great importance to take a cardiopulmonary resuscitation course (CPR), since that type of instruction teaches the importance of immediate assessment coupled with a need for immediate action.

Now to the business of assessment. We will deal with the three categories—social, psychological, and physical—realizing that they are interwoven and exist as a triad.

First, the social factors: a comprehensive social evaluation of the patient and the patient's environment is crucial to health assessment. While making a home call, look in the trash can and in the refrigerator; they may yield clues which are crucially important in making a diagnosis. Beer or whiskey bottles coupled with an empty refrigerator suggest vitamin deficiency diseases may exist—and, in fact, may explain continuing weight loss which was not evident when seeing the patient in a clinic situation. Environmental factors—fleas, mites, or other unsanitary conditions; lack of heating—are some of the many important fir lings which can assist in treatment of a failing elderly patient. Relationships with neighbors, friends, and immediate family—all of crucial importance—can be discerned just from evaluating the living situation. The existence of a large number of animals, dead or alive, or the harboring of garbage from months past (as is often seen in paranoid patients) can be additional clues for making medical diagnoses.

Psychological factors also emerge. Often elderly, depressed, and/or demented patients sequester themselves in their rooms because of marked paranoid ideation. It is then impossible to give adequate medical or psychiatric help. Accurate evaluation of relationships between family and patient are crucial, because without the cooperation of the family a treatment plan often cannot be adequately carried out. Other important assessments of the patient's psychological state relate to the individual's orientation to time, place, and person. Thus, when encountering a new patient it is quite easy to overlook a significant degree of mental deterioration or psychotic behavior unless the patient is placed in a somewhat stressful situation and asked specific questions which reveal the mental status. Some patients with organized delusional systems actually appear quite rational until the delusional system is touched upon and subsequently explored.

Now for some physical assessment procedures. Since we are discussing primarily emergency and semi-emergency situations, it is fundamentally important for the observers to have their wits about them at all times. Persons who have run half a block in response to screams can hardly be expected to make a reasonable assessment until they themselves have stopped, taken a deep breath, counted to five, and begun to work. In teaching people how to do effectively cardiopulmonary resuscitation, I have found that a three- to five-second break for the observers permits them to gather their wits and is of critical importance.

Checking the vital signs is the most immediate task to be performed. Measurement of the patient's pulse, blood pressure, and respiratory rates is fundamental information to be relayed to the physician. Thus, continued practice in taking the pulse both apically (just at the heart) as well as radially (below the thumb at the wrist) is of great value. When describing the vital signs it is also important to note whether sweating, change in color, or any other significant abnormality is present in the general condition of the patient.

Following this, special attention is paid to the skin. A

quick search for bruises, areas of hemorrhage, evidence of trauma such as laceration (or in more extreme circumstances, the site of knife or bullet entrance or exit wound) should be made—all are important. The sudden appearance of a rash coupled with collapse of a patient who has recently been treated with penicillin could suggest an acute penicillin reaction; just the information about the rash could give the physician the information necessary for initiation of proper, appropriate treatment.

Swelling of the legs or coldness of a particular part of the body (often a leg) can be a clue to abrupt interruption of circulation. Other forms of skin abnormalities become esoteric and are not important at the initial semi-emergency evaluation session.

Following skin, the assessment of the orthopedic system is important. When faced with an elderly person lying comatose on the floor, one immediately has to look for signs of fracture, particularly fracture of the hip. In fact, if a person lying on his back has one foot straight up and the other foot rotated so it is virtually flat on its side on the floor, one can strongly suspect the existence of a fractured hip. Again, swelling of a particular joint associated with marked weakness and fever could suggest a massive bacterial infection of the joint and the need for immediate hospitalization and treatment. Additional orthopedic emergencies are fractures of the spine, wrist, arms, and legs. Trauma to the face, which often occurs with a "sinking spell," must be looked for very carefully, particularly if bruises around the eyes are noted. In fact, any evidence of trauma must be searched for and recorded. We have had cases where patients have fallen and sustained rather significant injuries within the brain, although these injuries took from a few days to weeks to manifest themselves.

Neurologic assessment can be done rather quickly and is of immense value to the distant physician. A rudimentary neurologic examination can be accomplished even by a relatively unskilled person within two minutes. For example, asking the patient to use each hand to squeeze yours can immediately demonstrate whether function exists in the hands; asking the person to "make a muscle" in both upper extremities rules out paralyzing stroke in these limbs. A similar type of examination of the lower extremities, where flexion of the legs at the hip is tested, bespeaks good neurologic function in both lower extremities. Assessing the ability to walk, talk, smile, and laugh can comprise the remainder of the examination. Anything more involved—reflexes, sensory findings, etc. —is beyond the scope of this discussion.

The cardiovascular system is responsible for the majority of emergency and semi-emergency situations that can occur. Heart attacks, cardiac arrhythmias, or congestive heart failure are some of the major events that can occur precipitously. Evaluation is rather simple. It requires taking the pulse both radially (in the hand at the wrist, below the thumb) and apically (just beneath the breast on the left side), counting the pulse for one full minute, and noting whether it is regular or irregular (if irregular, note the pattern of the irregularity). The discovery of an irregular heart rate, be it fast or slow, can be of invaluable assistance to the physician in making a determination as to the cause of any cardiac event.

It is important to evaluate the breathing rate, whether breaths are deep or shallow, and what associated sounds are made which accompany breathing. Sighs at the end of an expiration are generally related to anxiety states, whereas wheezes or other sounds emanating from the chest are generally indicative of an underlying pathological condition. If the person has been coughing, it is important to examine the sputum. Evidence of discoloration, particularly green or yellow, indicates infection; red or dark brown often indicates bleeding within the pulmonary system.

The legs should be evaluated for edema (swelling) by placing the second and third fingers over the skin in the lower leg and noticing how deep an indentation, if any, is made.

Another diagnostic area is the feet. Foot problems can represent an emergency situation. Patients heretofore able to shop and care for themselves will find their whole pattern of existence in jeopardy if unable to walk because of foot problems. Signs of infection, abscess, or vascular problems represented by a cold, cyanotic (blue), painful foot are true medical/surgical emergencies and need to be reported to the patient's physician as soon as possible.

Other emergency or semi-emergency problems can involve the eyes. Since glaucoma is most prevalent among older persons, the possibility of acute glaucoma attack with severe pain in the eye accompanied by redness and tenderness can represent a true emergency, which if not treated can result in the loss of the eye. Other problems include injury to the eye from a foreign object and secondary infection; these too must be dealt with on an emergency basis.

These are some of the essential details of a health assessment program for the elderly specifically concerned with emergency and semi-emergency problems. As mentioned earlier, a future publication will describe assessment of the more routine, standard problems in depth.

It is of critical importance that all health professionals— social workers, nurses, speech therapists, physiotherapists, etc.—be aware of the physical changes in the elderly that accompany underlying medical and/or surgical problems. Very often it is one of these persons who has the first encounter with the patient and can play an important role in the future health care of the individual.

Physiological Changes That Influence Patient Care

2

Ruth B. Weg, Ph.D.

Over our history changes with time and the signs of aging have made a painful impression upon many a human imagination and have given rise to a great variety of interpretations. There is something prophetic about one of the Beatle songs:

> "Will you still need me
> Will you still feed me
> When I am sixty-four
> You'll be older too ..."

There is little doubt about the data emphasizing the reality of generalized physiological decrements with age, but no one individual represents the average and not all known dysfunctions happen to the same individual. In your conversations with older people you must have noticed the wide range and the variability of relatively normal functioning. What are the bases for the cliche of the older person as a senile, chronically ill, bedridden end-stage human being?

If I had to choose a phrase that described my commitment to the field, it would be "aging without pathology." As you can guess there has been insufficient attention given to this concept of normative aging and so there is insufficient normative data. Is it not conceivable that much of the data regarding older persons is misleading? Physiological comparisons and measurements have been arrived at using young adult values as the yardstick. Is it necessarily true that "feeling well" in the case of a 25-30 year old person and a 90 year old person cannot have the same connotation? Is it not conceivable that abnormal states (for blood pressure, glucose levels, etc.) for young adults also represent features of pathological old age rather than normal aging? It is possible that some values which are close or equal to the optimum values in young persons represent the normal limits of old age as well. It may be that the altar to youth of most western cultures, our own included, has distorted our expectations and our behavior toward the aging of others and ourselves.

I like the World Health Organization's definition of health. Health is defined not as absence of disease but as the state of total physical, psychological, sociological, and enviromental well being. This kind of outlook stresses the importance of separating "normal aging" from the pathology so long identified as "aging."

Let us examine some of the real differences between young and old, and their significance for us. The metabolic disturbances we call diabetes illustrate the difficulty in distinguishing clearly between biologically normal aging, pathological aging, and disease. Older persons with a so-called "diabetic type" of glucose tolerance test show no evidence of diabetes on clinical examination. In fact, the blood glucose values in the fasting state may be quite similar in young and in the aged. The difference may only show up under specific stressful circumstances (as in the glucose tolerance test). Hypothermia is another example of the decreased homeostatic capacity of the aged person. It is a real danger for the aging, since adjustment to excessive temperature and temperature changes is less rapid and less effective. These changes point to one of the more dramatic differences between young and old. The dominant challenge for the aging organism is to maintain integrative functioning of the nervous system as the capacity to re-adjust to change decreases. Indicative of aging is the measurable change in the ability of the organism to maintain homeostasis in the coordinated activity of a number of organ systems.

What is the evidence for aging processes? What do we see when we look at an aging person? Without the pathology, what are the critical functions at risk with time? In the old, as in the young, muscles contract, nerves conduct, and secretion continues. What are the changes then?

There is no universal acceptance of particular cell abnormalities as clear evidence of intrinsic age changes. If we can identify specific changes, we are unable to establish a cause and effect relationship. For example, aging pigments (lipofuscin) build up in cardiac and nervous tissue. These may occupy up to 4/5 of the cell volume, yet function does not appear to be significantly hampered. It is possible, however, that beyond a certain point such cells die. This may keep us unaware of the important consequences of age pigments.

There is good, reliable evidence for many of the following phenomena underlying typical concomitants of increasing age:

1. Cell death is a time-related phenomenon of probable influence and significance in the physiological manifestations of aging.

   (a) The loss of cellular units by death in skin, blood, liver, gastro-intestinal tract, and bone marrow is partially compensated through replacement. However, the rate of destruction may exceed rate of replacement with increasing age.

   (b) The loss of cellular units in the CNS, muscle, and kidney is representative of loss in the kinds of cells that no longer have the power of cell division or regeneration. These may be most crucial in the aging processes. In the nervous system, for example, the functional neurons may be replaced, but by non-functional glial cells. So we are talking about death of units and decrease in function of those that remain.

2. There is good agreement that there are changes in fibrous proteins. Elastin fibers become thicker and aggregate, and are less elastic. The collagen fibers

become less soluble. These changes in turn influence the structure and composition of the skin, the vasculature, and those very important joints.

3. There is good evidence for changes in mineral metabolism. Calcium, for example, under dietary and hormonal changes may leave the bone and invest the soft tissues. It may enter into the lining of arterioles and into the joint sacs, leading to narrowed blood vessels and pain. Stiffening the rib joints, there may be increased difficulty in breathing. Changes in the bone structure may cause reduction in height, the familiar stooped posture, and limitations in mobility —all earmarks of advanced years.

4. There is a measurable, progressive reduction of basal oxygen consumption by the aging person. This reflects the lowering of reserve in all body functions Since we can only do that for which energy is available, we can't do as much as we get older. For example, necessary syntheses of the stuff of protoplasm decreases. More biochemical studies would provide information to substantiate these changes of time, exercise, and disease. Research could demonstrate the reduction in available oxygen and in the use of O_2 even when it is available. The more molecular information we can gather, the closer we may come to a real understanding of basic aging processes.

5. There is evidence for measurable change in heart and blood vessel structure and function. Blood vessels narrow to cause increased peripheral resistance. Blood pressure increases with age, and can be modified by environmental, genetic and cultural factors. There is a decrease in the capacity of the heart to respond to extra demands, to the stress of heavy work, and to emotional tensions. Any sclerotic changes in vessels of the brain may contribute to identifiable psychological symptoms.

6. We know that breathing may be less efficient due to changes in the muscles of the ribs and chest, arteriosclerotic changes in lung blood vessels, changes in

elastic fibers, and/or changes in rib joints. As a consequence, less oxygen is available to reach all tissues of the body.

7. There is evidence for changes in the gastrointestinal tract. A number of frequently cited physical factors attest to this. There is a decrease in sense of smell and taste, a loss of teeth, problems with dentures, a reduced motility of stomach and intestines, a reduced secretion of digestive juices, constipation, hemorrhoids, malnutrition, and a decrease in fluid intake. Unfortunately, there is an increase in the desire for and consumption of sweets. Often this is in the role of fulfilling psychological needs, rather than essential hunger.

8. There is agreement that changes in the genitourinary tract present the aging individual with new concerns and threats to his dignity and personality. There is an increase in urinary incontinence and in frequency of urination. With men, this is often related to the enlargement of the prostate. With women, this is often accompanied by infection of the urethra or the bladder. Atrophic changes of genital tissues in men and women are expected changes with time. Natural involutional changes accompany the decrease in gonadal secretions and lead to a gradual atrophy of vaginal tissues after menopause, a decrease in lubrication, and a decrease in the size of uterus and cervix.

9. Some of the other endocrine glands also come in for gradual, measurable changes. There is a marked decrease in the ability to fight disease as well as an increase in autoimmune properties. This loss of recognition of self often leads to the destruction of one's own tissues.

10. There are notable changes in the nervous system, the chief coordinating, integrating mechanism of the human body. Reaction time and speed of movement slow down. This effect is common to different sensory modalities and several different motor pathways.

Simple neurological function which involves few connections in the spinal cord remains virtually unchanged. It is the complex connections of the central nervous system that aging appears to affect mostly. contributing to memory loss, to difficulties with decision making, and to the decrease in homeostatic capacity. In any parameter we choose to monitor—heart rate, blood pressure, resistance to infection—the magnitude of the displacement is greater and the rate of recovery is slower.

11. And finally we find empirically that there is an increased susceptibility to disease, particularly chronic disease. There appears to be a statistically significant increase in death from causes that earlier in life would not have had this result.

As we age and accumulate these changes in structure and function, it would appear that there is little left to work with. But is it necessary to maintain the strength and speed of youth into the sixth, seventh, or eighth decades? It may be that there is more than sufficient capacity left for the life style of the older person.

Here is a sketch of the "mythical older person" which exists in the minds of helping professionals and the community at large. First, all older people have advanced cases of arteriosclerosis. Therefore, all of them are senile. Don't bother to engage them in any decision making, large or small. Treat them gently, as you would children. Second, all older people have lost interest in eating. Their senses are dulled and their digestive systems are dysfunctional. What's more they are either constipated or diarrhetic. Don't worry about presenting them with a well balanced or attractive meal because it just doesn't matter. Third, all older people are in advanced osteoarthritic states. It's painful for them to move, so keep them still and in bed. Fourth, all older persons over fifty haven't (or shouldn't have) any interest in their sexuality. They have little physiological capacity for a normal sex life. Accept their sexual incompetence, and discourage conversation or interest in this regard.

These are myths about aging we need to do away with.

Older people are not all alike and they are not like these myths would have us believe. More probably, as people age, differences in behavior and personality may be enhanced as the variety of life styles comes to a full and ripened relief. Reviewing these myths, they do not seem to adequately characterize the elderly person.

Arteriosclerosis is not equal to aging. It is a pathological process that can begin at any age. It is more related to dietary patterns, occupational stress, genetic history, and total life style than to age alone. In some situations, markedly reduced blood to the brain in extremely sclerotic blood vessels will contribute to a blood starved brain and consequent senile behavior. In an equal number of cases, however, the senility is really pseudosenility. It is a reflection of an imposed withdrawal from reality and not impaired circulation. Often this has proven to be reversible, with "Tender Loving Care" related to nutrition, friendship, and engagement with the world.

Nutrition is not less important for the aging person. While it is true that taste, vision and smell may indeed decrease with age, the need for adequate nutrition is even more acute in the aged than in the young. Since there is less leeway and less reserve available in the generally contracting organism, regular meals become extremely important.

Movement is essential for painfully stiff joints and muscles. Bone and muscle changes with time can be an inconvenience, leading to decreased mobility, increased pain and increased irritability. These symptoms call for greater movement, for regular exercise, for a fight against disuse contributing so crucially to the atrophy of muscles and joints.

Sexuality is natural at any age. A recognition of this fact for the 50-70 year age group is essential. There is no excuse for confusing symptoms of sexual dysfunction (possible at any age) with the physiological changes associated with time. It appears there are only two basic requirements for regularity and satisfaction in sexual expression in the 60-90 year group: a good state of health and an interested and interesting partner! Studies by Masters and Johnson as well as those at the Center for the Study of Aging and Human Development at Duke have provided considerable supportive examples.

What are the implications for care, as we attempt to keep separate frank pathology from the normal variations due to aging processes? If the helping professions accept the goal of achieving, maintaining, and/or recovering the state of health for all people put in their charge, a critical question is raised: "What can I do to maximize the capacities that are left, to realize and extend the potential that exists?"

The elderly need care, but usually their needs are greatly exaggerated. The fear of being ill and the fear of the unknown leads most patients to look for a confidant who is a part of this "new home away from home." They need someone who can reassure, listen and advise, and who can offer human warmth and intimacy. The elderly are the "deprived minority" at an extreme, experiencing not only physiological losses but also the loss of friends and family and the loss of substantive roles in society.

A considerable number of adjustments are required of the patient. There are sudden demands that they give up personal material—their money and jewelry, for example. This assaults their sense of identity. The sudden impersonalization of a strange, crisp, non-human, unfamiliar environment would push the limit of any individual's coping capacity for change and decrease in significant human companionship. Accumulated anxieties concerning what has been left behind —home, job, mate, children, grand- and great-grandchildren —reflects the fear of loss of control and connection with the past.

When a "person" becomes a "patient" multiple inroads on the individual's privacy are compounded. There are the first day measurements, the history, the examinations—all done on a business-like, unemotional level. The small regard for individuality or privacy is reflected in the sameness of each room and each corner of the room. There are the losses of independence and of self-identity. Few patients are consulted for their suggestions about changing the procedures or scheduling of institutional routines.

What really goes on in treating the elderly? The nurses, pushed to the limits of time and energy and confused about their real role as helping professionals, try to let the hospital system protect them from emotional involvement with patients. To insulate themselves, nurses treat patients all alike, though in fact each is an individual. Nurses also seek anonymity through the uniforms they wear. This is contrary to what is humanly desirable—a warm interpersonal relationship in which the older patient can trust in the nurse with reasonable expectation of acceptance.

In view of the individual and human requirements of the older patient, nurses may be helped by these guidelines:

Nurses may be able to help make eating an exciting adventure and to maximize the possibility for at least adequate nutrition. There is reason to expect improvement in the patient if he eats well.

Nurses can stimulate participation in simple physical activities which may determine whether the patient leaves the hospital or nursing home on his feet instead of on his back. Nurses might take the time to walk with their patients or to develop simple exercises and other kinds of physical activities. A whole new self-image may grow as a patient discovers a new control over his physical being.

Nurses need to encourage their patient's sense of self and self identity. Individual attention can help bring about the involvement of a patient in his exercise regimens, eating, interpersonal interaction, and future plans. Planning *with* the patient, not for him, can potentiate useful alternatives not yet contemplated.

Nurses may need to throw out their own hang-ups about sexuality so they can encourage an expression of normal libidinal urges in their aged patient. Sexuality is but one aspect of human affect, and an important way to realize self and personhood.

Nurses need to take time to know the individual patient. Nurses need to deal frankly with anxieties and with the fears of the chronically ill. Nurses need to be able to face with the patient the end of life, the coming of death. They can help the individual to review the years, the deeds, the things to be done, to resolve the doubts, and to make the most of each day.

What needs to be known? How can we be in a better position to help old people in sickness and health, to stretch the vigorous years beyond the 40's? How can we learn to see the older years as a time, not of disease, but of changed but useable capacities?

The studies on aging to date are characterized by a large measure of unreliability. Why? Often young and old differ along other dimensions than simply that of age. In cross-sectional studies, comparing varied young groups with old, the old are often chronically ill and institutionalized, whereas the young are mentally alert and healthy. Therefore, not only age differences, but physical and mental pathology become relevant. The result is bad data and invalid inferences.

There is difficulty in establishing standards of normality for glucose tolerance tests, serum cholesterol or triglyceride levels, arterial blood pressure, and clinical pulmonary function tests. There are no independent sets of standards for each age group. The hope for age-standardized tests rests with longitudinal studies like those in progress at the Gerontological Research Center at Bethesda, The Fels Research Institute for Study of Human Development at Antioch, and the Center for the Study of Aging and Human Development at Duke University Medical Center. Differences between young and old individuals may be reflected, not in any obvious, large qualitative differences, but in subtle changes permitting relatively normal function with time.

We need to have records in these longitudinal studies of age, individual rates, variations and decrements in height and weight, increases in chest depth, changes in the amount and distribution of body components, and also measures of changes in speed, strength, and range of motion. We need further descriptive data regarding changes in special senses and in neurological functions. We need multivariate analysis, since all organs do not age or change with time at the same rate. We need to begin to know which measures provide good indices of chronological or physiological age, such as changes in visual accomodation, dark adaptation, graying of hair, elasticity of skin, or a combination of several of these variables.

Most of this information is necessary, or at least useful, in the design of housing, furniture, hospital supplies, and automobiles. It is needed to determine fitness of individuals as drivers of autos, pilots of planes. It is needed for structuring programs in educational and occupational rehabilitation. There are other ways, perhaps more important, to use this wealth of data. Research can increase our understanding of what aging is, and ultimately ought to help us predict aging. We would detect subtle changes indicative of frank pathology early. We could identify those who will age more slowly as well as individuals at risk. Perhaps we will be able to intervene and change the course of events.

To summarize, although decrement is the watchword for the older person, this loss need not bring about significant morbidity. Losses need not consign the aged to the "to be discarded" group. Today's technology has reduced the requirements for even the young to possess the strength and speed of earlier days. Society has played (and still does) a "stressor role" by setting unreal and unnecessary "youth" standards for older persons. Finding the aged wanting, we reject them (and our future selves) as unsuccessful and undeserving.

Aging individuals (1) do not need to run up and down stairs 4-5 times per day; (2) do not need to run (or jog) from home to store or job; (3) do not need to lift packing cases of supplies; (4) do not need to change a tire or shovel snow off the drive.

Many older persons perform many of these tasks, and at comparable rates with younger adults. The normative life styles of our society certainly make no such requirements, however. Older persons *do* have to be able to think, make decisions, plan and imagine, maintain interpersonal relations, have a close friend to touch and be touched by, contribute, and be aware of a changing physical and human world. Yes, the aged need to be human too!

What has this to do with nursing? Everything! If we agree that the state of health is the psychological, sociological, and physiological well-being of the individual in interaction with his environment, then the nurse may be the most crucial other individual around who can help the aged person realize the best health possible and maximize the quality of the time left.

Since the older people of tomorrow will no doubt be different, what do you think may be the most appropriate alternative suggestions for the health care of the aged? With the inroads in gerontology and the successes of medical research, we look to the next generations to be freer from degenerative disease. The major aging changes will start much later and proceed at greatly reduced rates. It isn't sufficient to measure what is and to be prepared for the brief today. The urgent step is preparation for tomorrow to plan for the old of the future who are the young and middle aged of today. They will be the beneficiaries of the revolution in biology and medicine today.

Psychological Changes That Influence Patient Care 3

Alexander Simon, M.D.

When the recommendations from the 1961 White House Conference on Aging are reviewed, one is impressed by the fact that essentially the same problems are still being faced some years later. We have made some progress, but far from enough. In fact, Medicare and Medicaid legislation have brought to view problems and issues that once were hidden— problems related to the administration and delivery of health care services, suicide among the aged, alcoholism, nutritional problems, economic support, isolation, housing, transportation, and protective and supportive services of all kinds. Other problems now made more visible include the inadequacy of methods for providing continuity of care, the lack of provision for comprehensive health care in various institutional settings within the community, and the relative failure of the community mental health centers to provide comprehensive care needed by the aged. We know that health care for the aged should include diagnosis, treatment, and rehabilitative care to help individuals to maintain or return to as high a level of physical and mental health as possible, and this should include the active participation of the individual to the greatest extent possible, considering any handicaps that may be present.

We need programs especially for the isolated, the minorities, foreign-speaking groups, and the rural aged. We need trained indigenous workers for these programs. We need close cooperation among professionals involved in physical and mental health care. We need a reduction in the fragmentation and duplication of services that now exists. We must recognize that the aged do not constitute a homogenous group, that there are differences between individuals in the 65 to 74 age group and those aged 75 and older. There are differences among the aged in various ethnic and socioeconomic groups. Aged patients in mental hospitals are not all the same, and they too require individualized treatment. In short, a variety of services is needed, from home care to institutional placement. Many of the aged need advocates and community aides who can assist them over the bureaucratic hurdles they often must face when trying to get needed help. There are therapeutic programs available and knowledge is available, but we need manpower, and that means more training. The quality of care must be improved, especially in facilities offering alternatives to hospital care. These services must be adequately supported with funding and administrative organization.

Having established this, I will try to define in a general way what the needs of the aged are and some of the stresses and losses from which they suffer. The needs of the aged person are like those of the younger person—to have friendships and social contacts, to be busy at work and play in keeping with his capacities, and to be in reasonably good health. Most older persons, although they may not always admit it, tend to reminisce, and in the process to try to understand what life has meant and what needs to be done before it is over. They need to feel that, all in all, theirs has been a good life. They want to feel they have made a contribution, that they have few complaints about themselves, and that others do not complain about them. They must accept their dependency needs realistically and live within their limitations. Not too many come up to this measure, but I am sure all of you know a number of old people who do.

I want to define a few terms. Nothing irritates me more than euphemisms such as "golden years" and "senior citizens" and such beautiful phrases that are used to avoid that threatening term "senility." In general, we refer to the age period 65 and over as the period of senescence without implying a deteriorating mental condition. The great majority of aged persons show few or no signs of memory defect or other evidence of intellectual deterioration. For those who do show varying degrees of such changes, a Montreal psychiatrist has suggested that there are two kinds of senescence, as indicated by memory changes. These are benign senescence and malignant senescence. Benign senescence is characteristic of the individual who is age 65 or over and who may be showing some mild memory defects. The process of deterioration is so slow that it is not easily observed except by detailed and critical testing. As a matter of fact, chances are that if the person lived to be 120, he might show some signs of deterioration but we could still call it benign senescence. The individual who exhibits malignant senescence is what has been called the "senile" patient, one who displays definite symptoms of confusion, disorientation, and memory defect. In such persons, the process of deterioration is likely to be rapid and considerable, and usually ends in death in a matter of months or a year or two.

There is a close correlation between the degree of psychiatric impairment in older persons and their physical health. Whatever the personal and individual stresses or the socioeconomic deprivations, physical health is the most important variable related to degree of psychiatric impairment in older persons.

From 1959 to about 1970, we at the Langley Porter Institute carried out a multidisciplinary study that provided much of the data I will discuss here. Our sample included all admissions to the psychiatric observation wards of the San Francisco General Hospital in 1959 who were age 60 and over and had not had any psychiatric hospitalization before age 60. The great majority of hospitalized aged mentally ill are admitted after age 65, and we wanted to study those psychiatric illnesses that are closely related to aging (in contrast to those that begin earlier in life and last into old age).

Of the 534 subjects in our sample, about 90 per cent suffered from organic brain syndromes, of which there are two broad categories, acute brain syndromes and chronic brain syndromes. An acute brain syndrome is an acute confusional reaction. Those of you who work in general hospitals and in nursing homes see many in this category, although they are not always recognized as such. When a patient who is age 65 or over enters a general hospital, no matter what his illness, the question of senility and cerebral arteriosclerosis arises. Attention is immediately drawn to the possibility of organic brain syndrome if the patient shows any signs of confusion or memory difficulties. It may be that he is suffering from a cardiac decompensation with a decreased oxygen supply to his brain, and so he has a transient confusional state. Nevertheless, if he is confused and is over age 65, the question of senility is seriously considered. That is nonsense. If his cardiac condition is treated, and if he becomes compensated and the oxygen flow to his brain returns to normal, his "senility" will disappear.

We learned in our study that almost half of the elderly patients who entered the hospital in acute confused states were suffering from an acute brain syndrome that was reversible. In some, this acute confusional state was superimposed on a mild to moderate chronic brain syndrome. In all likelihood, the neuropathologic changes had been developing for two, three, or four years, but had become exacerbated in the presence of a physiological decompensation. One of the most common ways this happens in a hospital or nursing home is that a patient is being given drugs. I have been in nursing homes where I believe all the patients were being given tranquilizers. There is something wrong with such a situation. Once you start giving any kind of sedative medication (even if it is called by the euphemistic term "tranquilizer") that has an effect upon the metabolism of the brain, you may precipitate an acute confusional state. This is especially likely in aged patients, and is easily mistaken for senility.

There are more or less malignant chronic brain syndromes in which the brain cells gradually die, and this inevitably leads to confusion, disorientation, and intellectual deterioration with progression to vegetative states. The most common chronic brain syndromes result from either senile brain disease, where there is a slow dropping out of nerve cells or cerebral arteriosclerosis, where a thrombosis occurs in the blood vessels of the brain—a stroke. We are not sure what causes senile brain disease, whether it is an accumulation of traumata from infectious processes over the years or whether it is an inborn genetic process. As the cells die, they are replaced by scar, and the brain becomes atrophied. In the case of cerebral arteriosclerosis, there may be a number of "silent strokes" with no evidence of focal damage. Or there may be just a fainting attack, when a small blood vessel is closed off. If there is an accumulation of these closures of blood vessels, there is a great deal of loss of nerve tissue and the end result is the same as in senile brain disease, considerable mental deterioration.

These are the two principal deteriorating processes in the aged, although there are other conditions that occur that may be mistakenly diagnosed as senile brain disease. Some of these conditions are the result of rare diseases that probably are of genetic origin, and some are the result of certain so-called presenile brain diseases such as Alzheimer's disease and Pick's disease. For the most part, however, chronic brain syndromes in the aged are caused by senile brain disease or cerebral arteriosclerosis, or by a combination of the two.

Older persons are subject to a great many stresses. In general, there is with aging a loss of vigor and loss of strength and coordination that are most meaningful to men, for obvious reasons. There are changes in appearance that are more significant to women. There is also an increase, with age, in visual defects and hearing defects that may lead to increasing isolation in older people. Especially with deafness there sometimes develops a paranoid reaction, which is understandable when someone cannot hear what is being said around him. The acute physical illnesses that characterized the hospital sample I spoke of were for the most part associated with heart disease, malnutrition, strokes, and serious respiratory infections. Lower on the list but still significant were cancer and peripheral neuritis, which is usually associated with chronic alcoholism. Of those 534 patients, 80 percent had severe physical illnesses that were serious enough to be disabling and would require hospitalization in a general hospital ward. Nevertheless, they were placed on a psychiatric ward because they were confused.

In addition, the elderly often suffer from a series of personal and socioeconomic losses. The effects of retirement probably have been greatly exaggerated. Retirement shock may last a few months to a year, but the great majority of people rapidly recover and are glad they are retired. (The same is true of widows and widowers; there is a shock, but it is recovered from in a relatively short time.) It is a myth that a large number of people die soon after their retirement. A great many retire because they are physically ill and they die from the illness that caused their retirement. A study has indicated that those who voluntarily retire live a little bit longer than those in the same age group who stay on the job.

I have underlined a number of physical, personal, psychological, and socioeconomic stresses that affect the elderly. How do they react to these? A good many of them deal with all of these stresses with an attitude of acceptance. These are usually individuals who have been more or less self-assertive, independent, and vigorous most of their lives. They accept the stresses and the losses without overcompensatory reactions or rationalizing behavior. There are some who do overcompensate, who have, particularly in the middle years, what we call "counterphobic" reactions, reactions against a fear of growing old. Their compensatory reactions tend to underline feelings of waning strength and, in the male, of diminished sexual potency. Women may exhibit more and more frantic efforts to look younger and younger in quite inappropriate ways. This group frequently makes exaggerated efforts to exercise. This counterphobic reaction is overcompensatory to the realistic fact that we just cannot be the same as we used to be.

There are still other ways to react to stress. Some deny that anything at all is happening to them. This can lead to serious consequences, as with the individual who refuses to wear a hearing aid or glasses, or who refuses to recognize that his vision is deteriorating and so allows glaucoma to proceed to the point of being irreversible, or who refuses to go to a doctor with early symptoms of diabetes. Many persons adopt this attitude because, they say, "I go to the doctor and he tells me it is all due to old age. So what's the use of going to him?"

Some react to aging with depression and withdrawal. A person brings with him into old age his past lifelong experiences and patterns of reaction and behavior. Even though no

overt symptoms of anxiety or depression may have been evident in younger years, under the stress of acute or cumulative
losses symptoms of depression or anxiety or somatic symptoms
may develop. There is a common but ridiculous notion that
anyone who shows a need to be dependent on another person
is somehow neurotic. But it takes a truly mature person to
recognize that he has a handicap and is dependent on other
people, and to accept that dependency without getting anx-
ious, depressed, or angry about it.

There are people who cannot blame themselves for anything. They project everything that happens to them upon
others. Everything is the fault of other people or of events in
the environment. A number of other old people react to the
stresses and losses that go with aging by exaggerating their
symptoms. They develop aches and pains in every organ, having what we might call an organ recital. Others are angry individuals who express their anger about changes that come with
aging not so much by lashing out against their environment as
by withdrawing from it. They give the world the silent treatment.

I will not go into the theories about patterns of aging.
For about ten years it has been fashionable to talk about "disengagement." Those of you who are interested will find this
theory discussed in numerous texts. The theory is that as you
grow older you gradually disengage, or withdraw, from involvement with the interests and activities in the world around
you. There is some validity to this, but it should not be misin-
terpreted to mean that you disengage from everything and become isolated. I know that I have begun to disengage in certain ways. About 20 years ago I decided that I had had enough
opera experience, and if I go once a year, that is enough. I do
not go the theater quite as much. I have all kinds of rationali-
zations, but it is part of a disengagement process. There is another theory that says the more engaged or active you are, the
better off you are. This may be true in the American culture,
but I doubt that it is true in all cultures, especially those with a
higher regard for older persons than we have.

Let us turn now to those older persons who are moderately or severely psychiatrically impaired, by which I mean

those who need some supervision and attention. The moderately impaired may need supervision or care for only part of the day or for certain activities. The severely impaired need 24-hour-a-day supervision or care. At the time we studied the group of hospitalized old persons, we also studied a sample of 600 old persons who lived in the community. These were matched to the hospital sample by such variables as sex, whether or not they lived alone, and socioeconomic status. We found that about 16 percent of those community-resident old people were moderately or severely psychiatrically impaired. They resembled in every aspect those old persons who had been admitted to the hospital.

We asked ourselves: what kept these people out of the hospital; why did the others get in? One of the main reasons the others got in was that they somehow came to the attention of some caregiver—a doctor, a nurse, a social worker, a policeman. They did something that drew attention to themselves. Once you have the attention of a doctor, nurse, policeman or the like who sees that you need help of some sort, something is going to happen to you. For these old people that something was likely to be hospitalization. Most of those who remained in the community were isolated to such an extent that they escaped attention.

Old persons who were living with their families came to attention much earlier in their illness because they behaved in ways that endangered their own health. If they did not follow the doctor's advice, that constituted a threat to their lives and tended to lead to hospital admission. The fact that they might have hallucinations or delusions was not really important. People in general will tolerate all kinds of strange ideas from old people because they think it is to be expected from them. But if their behavior is a threat to someone else or to themselves, as when they refuse medical care, then that becomes a reason for hospitalization.

The mental hospital is not the only place where mentally ill older patients are sent. In many states, and notably in California in recent years, we are sending severely mentally ill patients not to mental hospitals but to other kinds of institutions. We call these alternatives to hospitalization "care in the community." But we have not yet answered such questions as, is it better to treat such patients in nursing homes or in mental hospitals? Is it better to treat them in nursing homes or in boarding homes? Is it better to treat them in any of these institutions or at home? Some say that everyone should be in his own home. Well, they ought to try to take care of some confused, wandering, disturbed elderly person and see what it does toward the destruction of a family. The real question is not whether home care or institutional care is better, but what is the best place to treat the individual patient. It may be better to keep him at home. The family may feel they are willing to suffer many hardships in order to do so. Many of them do; too many do. Many would make that choice if they could receive some assistance.

And this is where the health care system in this country has utterly broken down. Medicare and insurance programs emphasize hospital care (but not in mental hospitals) and nursing home care, and treatment takes place where the money is. In spite of the talk about community care, the mentally ill aged are still in institutions, though these are nursing homes and boarding homes rather than mental hospitals. The emphasis on institutional care has meant that very little home care or protective and supportive services are provided.

At the time we carried on our study in San Francisco, more than two-thirds of the patients over age 60 who were admitted to the San Francisco General Hospital psychiatric wards were committed from there to state mental hospitals. That meant that the state hospitals had as many as five or six hundred aged admissions a year from there. Then, as a result of some of the findings of our studies in the mid-1950's, a social worker introduced a system of screening. Arrangements were made for old people to go to general hospitals or to general hospital psychiatric units, or to nursing homes or boarding homes, or to be kept at home, instead of going to the psychiatric observation wards of the San Francisco General Hospital. Within one year, the monthly admissions from that hospital to state mental hospitals dropped from 50 to 2.

The next question is, do these patients receive better care than they did in the state hospitals? We are substituting one institutional placement for another institutional placement, in most cases. A few of these alternative facilities are excellent, some are pretty good, but many are deplorable. The upgrading of these residential care institutions is essential, through improved financial support, standards for care and activity programs, and training of all kinds of personnel. Programs must provide the kind of care that gets patients out of bed and involved in activities, even if these are of the simplest kind. Many deteriorated, confused old persons can be helped a great deal. Many show signs of deterioration that is only a pseudo-deterioration. Left alone, inactive, with few or no visitors, and little stimulation and contact, they deteriorate through apathy. This loss of interest can cause them to be as confused and disoriented as if they had a severe chronic brain syndrome. When they are not allowed or encouraged to do things for themselves, many show what has been called "excess disability," that is, they seem much more disabled than their actual condition ought to make them. Rehabilitation programs can produce considerable improvement in such patients.

The most striking characteristic of older people is that of being extraordinarily individualistic. Each person is in himself the sum of all his days, of what he has done with them and what they have done to him. He is totally different from every one of his fellows, even from members of his own family who may have been exposed to the very same influences and events. All of us who are involved with the care of these old people should remember this when we are planning and carrying out programs and services that are meant to help them.

Needs, Environmental Design and Health Care of the Aged

4

Louis Gelwicks, A.I.A.

The question is often asked, "Why didn't someone ask a nurse when they planned this hospital?" Perhaps no one asked a nurse because nurses haven't made themselves heard by the right people. Where is the nurse who will speak up? I would like to encourage the nurses working in geriatric care to do that speaking up.

My work has involved a variety of programs and projects which include such diverse concerns as the preparation of a master plan for services and facilities for the aged in a Model Cities area, and a research project to bring together the very old and the very young in a combined nursing home and nursery school. All of these projects require good nursing consultation and expertise. Nurses who have the knowledge can be found, but those who are willing to speak up are not so easy to find.

There are some women in the field of nursing who have spoken up and have made significant contributions. Two nurses have addressed the issue of the nursing environment. One is Esther Lucille Brown in her book *New Dimensions in Patient Care*. The other is Florence Nightingale, who wrote *Notes on Nursing: What It Is and What It Is Not* way back in

1860. In one chapter she considers the notion of using color and form as a means of recovery.

> The effect in sickness of beautiful objects, of variety of objects, and especially of brilliancy of color is hardly at all appreciated.
>
> Such cravings are usually called the "fancies" of patients. Often their so-called "fancies" are the most valuable indications of what is necessary for their recovery. And it would be well if nurses would watch these so-called "fancies" closely.
>
> People say their effect is only on the mind. It is no such thing. The effect is on the body too. Little as we know about the way in which we are affected by form, by color, and light, we do know this, that they have an actual physical effect.
>
> Variety of form and brilliancy of colors in the objects presented to patients are actually means of recovery.

Here was a lady who really could observe people. She didn't have as much paperwork or technological gadgetry to distract her as does the nurse today. She observed patients and recorded her observations. My suggestion for all of us today is that we are losing our ability to observe. We don't take time for that anymore. We are not putting our thoughts down enough. We might profit by returning to this practice of observing, recording, and drawing conclusions to aid in structuring new ideas and approaches to our work.

In the area of environment, health, and aging, the nurse has a unique expertise. I believe her role and her obligation is to learn enough of the vocabulary of the other disciplines, particularly that of the planning discipline, so that she will not be hesitant to speak up. It's easier for the nurse to learn this vocabulary than it is for the architect, for example, to learn the nurse's vocabulary. This doesn't mean that the architect does not also have the obligation to learn this vocabulary as well, but I think direction and strength can come from the nurses.

A major problem in discussing environment and health is that the word "environment" is far too general. What environment are we talking about? Is it the physical environment, the social environment, or the psychological environment? This word is like "creativity" or "ecology." It means different things to different people. The meaning of the word depends on who you are, what you are, what discipline you come from, and what conceptual framework circumscribes your perception. These factors influence how we approach our environment and how we see it. The physical, psychological, and social environments interrelate, and, in fact, affect each other. We can't consider the physical environment without considering the social environment or the psychological environment. The meaning of "environment," then, embodies several approaches and several disciplines. It is important that we try to speak each other's language. Communication thus becomes the major point of focus.

The same communication problem surrounds the reality of aging. Aging doesn't just happen on our 65th birthday. There are different definitions of aging. Aging may be considered a process of closing out life's options. Aging is also a process of attempting to avoid closing out life's options. When we look at aging from these two perspectives we see that different things need to be done to increase the individual's capability of negotiating his environment. Unfortunately, what usually happens is that years are spent programming and putting together the "ideal environment" for aged persons. After four years of study and consultation this ideal facility is finally completed. Immediately after the building is in operation the staff that uses the building begins to complain. After a period of time, complaints to the administrator may subside. The expressions of discontent have only shifted to the nurses' station.

The questions, "Why didn't they ask a nurse when they designed this facility?" has to be asked before the building gets up. After it is in operation, it is too late. Most planners consider a program for building to be a list of spaces and equipment. Most design decisions are made on the typewriter, not on the drafting board. A list is probably the one thing that a program is not. A program includes channels of communications, people, activities, and a variety of other things. It is not just wheelchair space. It is at this stage the nurse's input is needed.

Technical standards must combine with other standards, those which emphasize environmental aspects. One of the ways of establishing a framework for discussion is to consider the elderly person as having a life space. Life space can be conceptualized to be the sum total of man's past, present, and future experiences which are relevant to his well-being. This life space consists of a series of sub-spaces or compartments: the personal space which he carries with him (the spatial distance which he keeps from other people), his primary and secondary living space (the spaces in which he sleeps and spends the majority of his time), his home range (that series of settings traversed and occupied by the individual in his normal activities), his physical world (that space which he believes he is capable of occupying either at present or in the future), and his psychological world (the inner as well as the outer world, limited only by his capacity for imagination).

Seen from within this framework, the patient's room eventually becomes his entire life space, particularly in an extended care facility. Moreover, this is the individual's last life space. Considering that the institution is the elderly person's life space, it is important to identify exactly which elderly person the environment is being designed for. It is certainly true that planners are not doing a very good job for the current elderly patient. If we move along in the same pattern, we will be doing a worse job for the patient of tomorrow. The elderly person of tomorrow for whom we are now planning an environment is, of course, the younger individual who enjoys an enormous life space. Think: this life space is going to contract to one room. Obviously this provokes a variety of questions. Who are the people who have to be designed for? What are their different needs? What activities will go on in these environments? What are the medical practices, procedures, and techniques that affect the design of this space? What are the prevalent building codes? Who are some of the people who influence the design of this room?

There are many things we can do with a patient's room. There are a variety of possible solutions to the particular situation, place, and patient. One of the things we do know from past research and from current research in the Andrus Gerontology Center is that for some strange reason people don't use rooms as they were originally designed to be used. For example, the semi-private room, which is supposed to provide more opportunity for social interaction, has been found to provide far less social interation than the private room. It seems that the individual who lives in a private room feels a sense of ownership. He demonstrates his "proprietary rights" by inviting others into his room. This patient socializes more than in the situations where the patients do not feel this environmental control.

One solution, designed to increase the environmental warmth in a "cold" institution involved replacing the traditional central nurse's station. The result was a highly dissatisfied nursing staff. Nurses were upset because they didn't have the nurses' station to use as a shield to retreat behind when the patients came up to initiate conversation.

Of interest to all of us dealing with older patients is one study about the adaptation and survival of the aged under stress conducted by Dr. Morton Lieberman at the University of Chicago. He looked at the population of a large facility which was to be demolished and the patients moved to different homes. What effect would this have on these people? What would be the effect of this change on their susceptibility to death? Over several years of observation it was found that after patients were moved to new facitiess the death rate went up 300%. A new, clean, stainless steel environment wasn't necessarily a better one for these old people.

Another study of centenarians shows in general and briefly that those centenarians who maintain a balanced perspective toward their past life and one in which no part of it is blotted out are those who are most physically and mentally well. There is a relationship between this and the hospital environment. To what extent are souvenirs, trinkets and furniture important in maintaining contact with past periods of our life? What kinds of significance do these things have for people? In hospital rooms, are there spaces for possessions? (Who would dare let you hang pictures on the wall of a hospital room?).

All details are important in the design of an environment. You, the nurse, must get involved in the design of future facilities. Demand to participate. Take courses in environment at the university. Lastly, be (or stay) emotional. Don't succumb to technocracy.

Recently I read a design directive done as a very small part of a three-year study on the design of pediatric hospitals in Boston. It read: "Do not install electronic communication where human interaction is essential!" Medical care of sick children requires a large amount of tactile and face to face communication. Electronic devices can only perform monitoring functions and cannot provide service and response to detected need. Young children are unable to use many of the adult communication devices. Electronic links tend to formalize communication. Also, the right of privacy might easily be violated by the use of electronic communication devices. I would say these remarks apply to the elderly person as well.

The Institutionalized Aged and Their Social Needs 5

Vern L. Bengtson, Ph.D.

The social context plays a crucial role in health. It is obvious that behavior and just about every aspect of living or dying is influenced by the real or perceived social context. I think the reason that we sociologists have so seldom been useful to nurses and practitioners is that there has been a tendency for each of us to stay safely within our disciplinary pigeonholes and to not look at what could be an important interchange between the scientific and applied worlds.

In this connection I think I can make my point most clearly by telling you the story of a 75-year-old man who was examined by a physician friend of mine and found to be in superb physical condition. My friend, who was a first-year resident and who had had very little acquaintance with elderly patients before, said to this fellow "I am really amazed at what good shape you are in. What's your secret? How have you avoided growing old?"

The old patient answered, "Well, I'll tell you. I've been married 52 years, and the very first day I was married I made a vow that every time I got mad at my wife, instead of lashing out at her, I would run around the block three times. At last count I have run around the block 4,832 times!"

The essential point of this story is that the rules and organization of this particular social dyad can influence the physiological condition of at least one of its members.

Having made that general point, let me go on to mention three needs which relate to the social context of older people. You can remember these three needs by the mnemonic device "ice" (I—C—E). These stand for three critical social psychological needs of elderly individuals. "I" stands for identity, something that we've already heard about. "C" stands for connectedness, connectedness in terms of the social situation in which we all live and die. "E" is a fancy social psychological term that is now just becoming popular, *effectance*. Effectance means having some sort of influence on your environment; being able to "effect" changes.

Identity. Connectedness. Effectance. These are psychosocial needs which operate throughout the life cycle. Parents of developing children learn about them as they watch their kids grow. Parents can see how their child's identity is formed, how important social connectedness is and how important having some effect on the environment can be. Practitioners and researchers working with aged individuals have tended to ignore the fact that these three factors are just as important in the aged as in childhood and youth. They are especially important for the dying patient.

I have said earlier that practically every aspect of living or dying is influenced by real or perceived social context. In the last ten years some imaginative studies have been conducted on the social context of death and dying. Many of you are familiar with some of these studies. One of the studies has been conducted over the years at the San Francisco Medical Center by Anselm Strauss and Barney Glaser. They have published their results in several books; among them are *Awareness of Dying* and *A Time for Dying*. What they have noticed is that a real social system operates around the dying individual over which he has little control. A patient comes into a hospital and is diagnosed as terminal. Formally or informally, the word gets around the ward that he's got two weeks, six weeks, or two days. You see this visibly in the reaction of the social environment when a patient outstays his time. What happens when an individual is admitted with a diagnosis of pulmonary pneumonia and the word goes out, "About a week," but then he stays for three months? You find the whole system of the hospital is somehow upset. What happens when a patient dies suddenly and very unexpectedly? What happens when a patient who is expected to linger on for a matter of weeks with terminal carcinoma dies two days after being admitted to the hospital? Suddenly the usual dormant mechanisms of self-examination in the hospital are called up. There are staff metings of the psychiatrists, the nurses, the doctors. All of a sudden elements of the social context become visible.

In our nursing homes I think we often forget that the same social connectedness, which formed a person's life, which gave it meaning and which gave him identity, is still important after he has been institutionalized. Moreover, the patient's will to live is rooted very clearly in his continued connectedness with a social system and in being able to have an effect on the world even in a nursing home. I would like to recommend that you look at a book by Irving Goffman. What Goffman does in *Asylums* is present a sociological perspective of what a total life institution is like. What we have to recognize is that we are dealing with individuals who are moving into institutions. And institutions invariably mitigate against the identity, the effectiveness, and the connectedness of individuals.

Aging has a negative image, but possibly this negative image of aging may be changing. In my research with age groups and different generational family members, it is very clear that the oldest and the youngest generation have a great deal in common. One might say that they are generation gap allies. Both are in effect dependent on the middle generation for a great deal of their emotional and possibly financial support. Both are discriminated against legally, occupationally, and economically—at least in our present-day society. Both are forced to make decisions about what to do with the time that their busy counterparts in the middle generation do not have.

One reason for this negative image of aging has to do with the lack of productivity of aged individuals. In our society and many Western societies, the worth of an individual has been measured either in terms of his productivity or his wealth. Why did we admire Grandma Moses? Because at the age of 80 she was still producing artistic things. Why do we not admire the little old lady who wants to sit in a rocking chair and do nothing? Because she is being unproductive! I suggest as a sort of teasing query: on what basis do you judge the effectiveness of the older people that you come in contact with? Our answer, of course, should be that effectiveness for the older person ought to be judged in terms of his frame of reference. Too often, we (as middle-class, predominantly middle-aged people) have attempted to use our own value system to define activities that are appropriate for aged individuals.

Let me conclude with some very practical guidelines. I suggest there are three things we should try to do in order to keep the identity, the connectedness and the effectance of aging individuals at an optimal level. First, we should try to experience the life space of the individual, especially that of the institutionalized older person. We should become familiar with them as people, as members of a group rather than as charges.

Second, begin to explore ways of changing the institutions which serve older people. Brainstorm with other staff about what is important to you in your life and what is important to older patients in their lives. Find out what you might do in the institutional setting (given the constrictions you are invariably forced to work within) to effect changes in the environment to increase patient's identity, connectedness, and effectance. So, the second thing is brainstorming with the rest of the staff.

My third suggestion—and the most important—is to examine your own perspective. Examine your own values with regard to aging and with regard to what is good and important and productive in life. From my own perspective, seeing an individual in terms of the things he makes, the money he earns, or the social status he attains is not nearly so important as his own experience of efficacy and fulfillment. Especially considering the goals and expectations of the various subcultures, there are very different ideals of what a good person is. If we try to lump all old people into one category, we are going to be doing them and ourselves a disservice.

Psychosocial Needs of the Aged in General Hospitals 6

Maxine Patrick, R.N., Dr.P.H.

In hospital nursing, as in much of nursing, a major area of care has always been in geriatrics. We seem to forget this and become upset with the continuing increases in the number of older patients in the general hospital. The changes in federal legislation have broadened the availability of health care through third party payment and have brought more older people into hospitals. The result is that the nurses must be concerned with the care of older patients. This requires that there be a constructive nursing service based on a realistic appraisal of the physiological functioning as well as the psychological functioning of these older persons.

It is important to consider the factors that help older people to maintain their mental and physical health. If a nursing service is one of the helping factors toward achieving this goal, and I believe it is, then we must realize that the older person is walking a physiological tightrope. The line between health and illness is a very slim one. Since physiological reserves of older people are limited, they must be protected and used carefully. For this reason, it would seem that the best thing to do is to keep the older patient out of the hospital. In the familiar environment of his home, he can cope. In a hospital, his mental health is impaired.

The necessity for maintaining the identity of the patient has been stressed. Nurses do this in several ways in the hospital. Taking nursing histories and developing nursing care plans are important for patient identity. Older people have established a style of life. Understanding and appreciating each individual's life style can help the hospital staff provide continuity and security to the patient. The more information we can obtain on admission, utilize in the nursing care, and transmit to others, the more successful we will be in preserving the patient's identity.

Diet is one particular area of life style that is easy to find out about. What is it the older person likes? What is it he usually eats? Too often older people don't eat the food the hospital serves. Poor nutrition can contribute to the mental confusion of older people. Knowing the patient's dietary preferences, he can be offered food that he is more likely to eat. I would also encourage nurses to work with the physician on special diet orders. Is this special diet really necessary? Maybe oatmeal three times a day for a short period of time is all he will eat. Is this really so nutritionally inadequate? How can his accustomed diet be supplemented? You cannot change the eating habits of elderly patients by prescribing a special diet that differs radically from what they are used to eating.

We are rejecting the patient's individuality when we ascribe our own values in making judgements for the elderly patient. Many times what we do (with the best intentions) is not at all what the patient wants. For example, most of us believe the maxim "Busy people are happy people." Some older people feel that retirement and old age have freed them from "doing things." Some of the things professionals think old people would like to do are viewed by these older people as busywork without meaning. Like anyone else, older people resent doing what is meaningless. They grew up and old believing in the Protestant work ethic. Arts and crafts and leisure time have never been a part of their life style. For them, a hospital is a place to rest and recover and not a place to "do" all kinds of things. Occupational therapy will not be therapeutic if the patient does not understand its purpose and resents forced involvements.

If the focus of the nursing care is rehabilitative, the family is automatically involved in this care. Families want to be involved. They want to help. It is possible to let them do something, and this can be something other than feeding the patient. If they feel they are helping, some of their guilt may be eased. The patient's family can do many things. They can take the patient out of his room for a walk or wheelchair ride to change the scenery. They can learn and practice those things they will do for the patient when he comes home. Remember that the family of the older patient is also confronted with problems. Often the children of the elderly are themselves moving into retirement and having to face their own old age.

Anyone caring for older people has to face the real possibility of death. What are your attitudes toward the need for expensive lifesaving heroics? How many times do you do cardiac resuscitation? Is a radical surgery really necessary? Families of the patients are requesting that they be allowed some part in these decisions. These are questions we must resolve for ourselves if we are to help others deal with these questions.

Another point frequently made by those dealing with older patients is the need to touch. The "dirty old man" concept is a false one, both from my personal view and from studies I have read. Both men and women have a need to touch and be touched. Older people, especially when they are ill, have fewer opportunities to satisfy this need, and may reach out to touch people who come close to them. When an old woman reaches out to touch someone it is tolerated. This same behavior in an old man is condemned. The one who is touched may be shocked. The touch is unexpected. Our non-verbal response communicates how we feel about being touched. Our reaction is usually a negative one. We often accompany our withdrawal with a verbal chastisement. Touching by an older patient is his request to be touched. It is a demonstration of his need for communication with another human being. If being touched unexpectedly bothers you, you can control the touching and still meet this need. Do this by touching the patient each time you come into his room. Shake hands or touch his shoulder. This lets him place his hand on yours if he desires and you can see the touch coming. Don't penalize old people (especially old men) who like to touch by not assigning young, pretty nurses to their care. Their behavior does not warrant this isolation, and you are only avoiding the problem.

Also, older people shouldn't necessarily be kept alone in a room, and they shouldn't be placed only in rooms with people of the same age. I think the old can learn from the young and the young from the old. In the usual hospital situation older people experience very limited sensory stimulation. The contact which they have with the staff is less frequent and of a shorter duration than that experienced by the younger patient. It has been found that the longer the over sixty-five patient is in the hospital, even if he is getting well, the more time he spends alone. This is the opposite of what happens to the young and middle-aged. Being left alone in a hospital room for hours on end certainly contributes to the sensory deprivation and mental confusion of the aged.

The plea I would make again is: work toward the reestablishment of optimal health so the aged patient can return home as soon as possible. The mental and physical health of older people will be maximized if they are at home. This must be the goal of hospital nursing.

Psychosocial Needs of the Aged in Nursing Homes

7

Elsbeth Kahn, Ph.D.

There are two basic fears that institutionalized elderly persons in particular have. The first fear is the fear of loneliness, the fear of dying in isolation. Very often a fear of dying is more a fear of being left alone and abandoned at the time of death. The second fear is more of a great anxiety over pending or actual loss of autonomy and self-direction. These fears can be partially alleviated or at least allayed by building a therapeutic environment in a nursing home. To do this some rather obvious things need to be considered.

First, there are the economic factors, the ways economic feasibility limits the planning possibilities. Nursing homes tend to cater to different socioeconomic groups. Those which accept mainly Medicare patients will have more limited services, particularly in the psychosocial area. Nursing homes that cater to a higher socioeconomic level deal with people from more affluent backgrounds. These people are likely to have more resources to deal with institutionalization. They have generally had free time to manage and have learned to keep active enough. Certainly this is not always true.

Regardless of a person's background, it is very important to find out what the person's style of life has been and what the person's interests are. This information will help nurses avoid pushing patients into activities which have never held any interest for them and certainly do not now. A nursing home experience can be a real crisis in an individual's life. It is important to provide some stability and continuity of life style for the patient. Recognize him as a person with certain past interests which can continue to have meaning in the present. It is the nurse's role to give the patient support and to provide him some opportunity to express some of his fears and anxieties.

It must also be recognized that there are always personal problems involved for those working with the elderly. Whatever personal reasons one may have for shying away from illness and death, these are supported by our culture which encourages us to ignore aging. This means we are encouraged to ignore a very important part of life. People working with the aged may learn about the process and problems of aging through their careers rather than in the course of their lives. This is due largely to the social context in which we live.

Many professionals are very keenly aware of what institutionalization means to the elderly person. Since there is very little we can really do to help, we turn away. We employ various kinds of social distance mechanisms for our self-protection from these aged. However, all of us must take some responsibility to heighten the social awareness of aging. This heightened awareness ought to be visible in social policy and in improvements in the institutional facilities and services for aged persons.

Nurses have a responsibility to bring about change. This requires that we understand both aging and our role with aging persons. We have a responsibility to promote attitude change and ultimately policy changes which will lead to the best distribution of resources for the aged. The nurse can play a part in preserving the dignity and identity of aged patients through her own relationship with them. She can involve others to expand this dimension of patient care. By allowing the patient to participate even minimally in planning for his own care and activities, nurses can help validate the patient as a person. Providing a continuity of life experiences whenever possible will serve this same purpose. Nurses can make a real impact in this area of care. It is important not to disrupt the lives of elderly couples who have to be institutionalized. There are many ways, if they both enter an institution, to keep them together. If only one of the pair has to be hospitalized, it is possible to make visiting and caring activities coincide. The well individual then can continue to have a caring relationship with the partner.

Adequate privacy is one of the fundamental factors which keeps patients functioning as well as possible in an institution. This is important when the nurse is providing care as well as at those times when a patient may wish to spend some time alone. Research suggests that when people are not allowed to perform autonomously and when they are not allowed to deal with stress in their own way, death can be the ultimate outcome.

One reason why working with the elderly is so difficult for us is that over and over we see our own futures mirrored. Although this is an unconscious perception, we are made very conscious as individuals that we could deal with aging much better. There is a real need for adequate social distance mechanisms to help nursing staff and other staff members cope with the pain they see daily. Particularly we need to learn ways of coping with the emotional pain of isolated and dying persons. It is one thing to work in a medical care setting where death occurs occasionally and where one is not constantly reminded of other problems of aging. It is quite another thing to be in a nursing home or extended care facility where mainly elderly persons receive care. Even the most mature professional person has limits to the support he or she can provide to a suffering person. But we tend to value continuity of care so that, for instance, one nurse gives total care to a patient. We never think about the tremendous cost to the nurse for this continuity. By planning care with an entire nursing staff, perhaps the most difficult aspects of psychosocial care could be equally distributed to all team members in keeping with their capacities. If we could recognize that we have psychological and emotional limits as well as physical ones, we would be willing to plan accordingly. Then we would perhaps require fewer psychotherapeutic sessions for our staff.

Finally, we must each be mindful of our obligation to help make life worth living. Life ought to be emotionally and socially rewarding if we are going to keep people living who have a reduced physical functioning capacity.

8 Psychosocial Needs of the Aged: What Nurses Can Do

Esther Lucile Brown, Ph.D.

What nursing can contribute to the aged, whether they are in institutions or at home, is tremendous. Nevertheless, so few nurses have been interested in cultivating programs for the aged that we have vast numbers of persons in long term institutions where there is poor physical care, where there is not even good custodial care, and where almost no attention is given to their psychosocial needs. I consider the role of nursing in planning, organizing, and administering services for the aged as well as in giving direct patient care so important that I recently spent much time looking at various facilities and programs.

The National League for Nursing asked me to travel around the United States to see what was new in nursing practice. What I found is reported in both Parts I and II of my book *Nursing Reconsidered: A Study of Change,* published by J. B. Lippincott, 1970 and 1971. In Part I, I discuss changes going on in institutional nursing, and in Part II, changes in community nursing. There are so many exciting developments in nursing that I could easily have overlooked what nursing was doing in the care of the aged. This specialty is so urgently needed, however, that I made a point to visit retirement homes with particularly promising programs. I also visited some of the better nursing homes for the aged, promising projects for senior citizens, and the program within the Veterans Administration. The Veterans Administration has now set aside four thousand beds in its hospitals across the country. They have created a physical and social environment as close as possible to that of a home and clubhouse for persons who had formerly been in "intermediate care." In this environment, nurses are in charge. Nurses selected for these units have available the services of physicians, dietitians, social workers, chaplains, and occupational and physical therapists. Nurses have been given the primary responsibility for planning how to set up these units and how to run a program that reproduces normal living as best as possible. It was assumed that the patients in these nursing homes (as they were called within the V.A.) would never leave until they died. In the first year nine percent of the V.A. patients improved enough so that they were able to move from the hospital to a foster home, back to their own homes, or to community nursing homes. The details of this program are included in Chapter 7 of *Nursing Reconsidered.*

Let us turn to another kind of care of the aged or disabled. It is concerned with those who want to stay at home, but who generally cannot because they need more help than a visiting nurse or public health nurse is able to provide. In San Francisco an organization called San Francisco Home Health Service uses 140 homemaker-health aides. These aides work under the teaching, direction, and planning of 12 nurses and 10 social workers. These 140 homemaker-health aides serve an average of 750 persons a month. If it were not for the aides these people would be in institutions. This program was created by a social worker some ten to fifteen years ago. At that time she believed she would never need more than twelve homemakers to meet the maximum requirements of the community. Although the agency is now using 140 workers, it is able to accept only one third of the requests for service since it has not been able to get the money to enlarge the program. Any sound program that can keep 750 people in their homes rather than in institutions is wonderful!

These were among the encouraging developments I saw. You can scarcely imagine how distressed I was seeing the things not being done. These things could be done readily if nurses participated in planning and operating programs. I saw new retirement homes with a minimum of provisions (or no provisions at all) for safety precautions, health care, or organized social recreation. Some had been built by churches. Why hadn't nurses, as members of the congregation of a particular church, formed a committee to advise the architect about what facilities need to be built into a residence for elderly people? When it is known that apartment houses for senior citizens are to be constructed with public funds, why don't nurses come forward and insist that health care, food service, social and recreational services be provided? Nurses must speak out, not only for nursing care, but for other services that are necessary for the aged. The elderly as well as the disabled are a population at risk.

This leads us to the subject of the psychosocial needs of the older patient. Their psychosocial needs are very largely like our own. Why, therefore, do we have such difficulty in defining them, thinking about them, or attempting to meet them? The basic problem is probably a social one. For a long time America has rejected old age. The emphasis has been primarily on youth, on activity, on obvious achievement, on getting ahead in the world. We have tried not to think about that stage of life to which we shall all come. We have acted as if it will not come to us personally. Our failure to perceive the psychosocial needs of the aged lies in part in this cultural rejection of old age and death. Our first step, therefore, must be to sensitize ourselves to our own psychosocial needs and then extend this sensitivity to the needs of older persons. Furthermore, we must resensitize ourselves continuously because otherwise we shall unconsciously slip back into rejecting the aged.

May I emphasize the importance of reading selected literature as a help in this process of resensitization. I should like to refer to two short articles in the *American Journal of Nursing*. The first article (December, 1969) is titled "Georgie." It was written by a young clergyman who went to a nursing home to see his uncle, who had been a remarkable man. He had been so dignified a man that few persons had ever called him by his first name. Yet everyone in the nursing home addressed him as "Georgie." The minister was pained to think that this wonderful man, at the end of his life, was only "Georgie" to a staff who knew nothing about him, who he was, or what he had done. The story is a plea never to call patients by their first names or even by such titles as "Grandmother" or "Grandfather" unless they ask to be addressed in that way.

Another article that appeared in the January 1970 issue of the *American Journal of Nursing* is by Irene Burnside. It is about the need for "Clocks and Calendars." Can you imagine being so forgetful of the needs of human beings as to fail to provide them with a clock or a calendar? These two items are an important part of our culture! Nearly everyone wears a watch. Nearly everyone would feel most uncomfortable going for 24 hours without looking at the time of day. Yet one can visit nursing homes for the aged across the country where there will be neither clock nor calendar visible. Some persons regain consciousness to find themselves in a home without knowing what day it is, or what month of the year. There is nothing to give them an answer to their questions, and frequently there are no staff who want to be bothered answering the question, "What time is it?"

A book I like is May Sarton's *Kinds of Love* published in 1970. The author has a rare ability to describe people with extraordinary perceptiveness. The setting of the book is a small town or village in New Hampshire. The theme is how that town preserves itself from generation to generation. Miss Sarton describes friendships, squabbles, young love, and middle-aged relationships. Most importantly, she describes a marriage that is emotionally fulfilled only after 30 years when the husband has already had a cardiovascular accident. Instead of his becoming "difficult," this successful Boston banker becomes more flexible and liberal in his ideas, more loving, and more companionable with his wife. Not all old age and not all cardiovascular accidents produce psychological damage!

An entertaining novel about a group of elderly people who live in a London hotel that caters exclusively to senior citizens is Elizabeth Taylor's *Mrs. Palfrey at the Claremont,* published in 1971 by the Viking Press. Mrs. Palfrey goes to the Claremont Hotel and discovers right away that one of the greatest needs of the residents is to talk about members of their families. They are all widows or widowers, and many are without children. Prestige is simply having a relative to talk about, especially one who comes to visit. So Mrs. Palfrey, when asked if she has any family answers, "Why, I have a nephew who is connected with the British Museum right here in London." What status it is to have a nephew on the staff of the famous British Museum! But the nephew fails to come to see his aunt. What do you think Mrs. Palfrey does? Thanks to fortuitous circumstances, she meets a bright, engaging young man, who is poor and badly dressed. She invites him to Saturday night dinners and shows him off as the nephew from the Museum. He is so delighted to have a good meal once a week that he agrees willingly to the deception.

Next Mrs. Palfrey writes to her sister in Scotland, who doesn't come to see her either. To show her sister how well she is getting along, she reports that she thinks she will remarry. (One of the men living in the home has actually asked her to marry him, but she has no intentions of accepting him.) The sister promptly gets in touch with her son, Mrs. Palfrey's real nephew. She tells him to go right away to see his aunt. "We can't let Auntie get remarried; some man will get all the money!" So Mrs. Palfrey winds up with two nephews. I'll not tell you the outcome as I hope you will want to read this delightful tale.

Let me refer to one more book that is so remarkable it is worth the struggle of trying to find a copy. *The Big Ward* was written by the Dutch novelist, Jacoba van Velde, and was published in 1960 by Simon and Schuster in a magnificent translation. Although it has been translated into at least ten languages, it is difficult to find because bookshops in this country ask "Who wants to read about an old lady in a nursing home?" It is the story of a Dutch widow who found herself one morning in a nursing home. She had had a cardiovascular accident. She did not know where she was, or why, or what season of the year it was. Later she learned she had been admitted to a home. This is a simple, very moving account of how she feels about life in a good nursing home. It is equally an account of how her daughter feels who comes from Paris to see her. One of the greatest burdens both for the mother and the daughter is the lack of privacy. There are no private rooms and no small lounges. Everywhere there are patients, who are so lonely that they want to share any visitor who arrives.

Listen to what the daughter thinks to herself after she leaves her mother for the return to Paris:

> What a sad parting! She tried so hard to hold back the tears—right up to the very last moment. And all those persons who were sitting around us! Why didn't they have the decency to go away? They can't, of course; they only have their dormitory. "I shall try to come again soon, Mummy," I said. "To be sure," put in Miss Laus. "She'll be coming back. You don't need to upset yourself so much." "Naturally, it's terrible for your mother that you are going away," whined Mrs. Jansen. "When are you due in Paris?" asked Mrs. Blazer. I cursed them all. I should have loved to scream at them, "Go to the devil!" But I said nothing. I sat in front of my mother on the high plush chair. We loved each other helplessly.

These are a few of the psychosocial needs, particularly of those persons who live in institutional settings. A very important need is for continuity of life experience. This includes a recognition of the individual's past, of the living present, and of a future toward which to move. Even when ties with the past have been cut through loss of family, friends, and home, the keeping of a few cherished possessions can be encouraged, former skills and interests can be revived, familiar cultural rites cultivated, and acknowledgement made of past achievements. Looking toward the future can be encouraged through involvement in a dynamic present which is always changing. Those persons who say that they "just can't die" because they would be "afraid of missing something," truly exemplify this continuity of life experience.

A second need that must be encouraged at all costs is self-identity. Residents need the opportunity to identify themselves by being gently encouraged, if necessary, to tell about their interests, former work, hobbies, ancestors, grandchildren, and what not. Nurses often claim they are too busy to spend time in conversation with residents or patients. Volunteers can be of great help not only in talking with and listening to residents, but in introducing residents to one another and in helping to promote the formation of congenial groups.

The maintenance of a sense of independence is also of great importance. A chief complaint among the old generally is that they are not permitted to decide or do things for themselves. Because institutions tend to be very restrictive, a conscious effort needs to be made continuously to encourage self-direction, freedom of choice, and movement as much as possible.

Reference has already been made to the need for privacy which is essential to the self-respect and well-being of each person. Almost equally important is the need for a sense of stability and of territorial possession. Instead of assigning a person to a bed and moving him to another bed or room without even discussing the matter, the patient should be as free as possible to choose his own room, his bed, and his roommates, and also should be assured about the permanence of his choice.

Some of the retirement homes, with their carefully considered programs, underline their recognition of the importance of meaningful living. They may furnish a prospectus of the social and cultural facilities available in the neighborhood. They may also have a list of the committees considered important to the functioning of the retirement home or for offering services to outside organizations. Asked to check a preference for serving on the hospitality, bridge club, holiday festivities, or library committee, the resident is assured services will be welcomed and that an active and stimulating environment will be provided.

In nursing homes, the resident is more likely to have nothing expected of him—no task or responsibility. He is seen and sees himself as not "productive" in any sense. Yet many of these same persons are physically or mentally able to do things that would reactivate former interests and skills. These activities might be symbolic of the activities of the productive years, and provide them with more meaningful living and a sense of self-importance. A resident can make his bed or dust his room or assist the cook with simple tasks. He can read to other residents no longer able to see the print. He might be given responsibility for guiding slightly disoriented persons. He could plan parties, serve coffee to visitors, or play games with the children. A resident could knit scarves for boys' clubs or make stocking dolls or stuffed cloth animals to send to the children's units of public hospitals. He could play grandparent to small groups of visiting children in need of affectionate attention. Or, he could help with their reading, spelling, and arithmetic. Efforts such as these, if encouraged and given recognition, will not only help the resident maintain the feeling that he is important because he is useful, but such activities will contribute immeasurably to another psychosocial need—the will to live.

9 Psychosocial Needs of Older Adults in the Community

Valerie L. Remnet, R.N., M.S.W., L.C.S.W.

As service providers in the community, we work with older adults in their own environments. This provides us with the opportunity to learn the uniqueness of each elderly person, observe how he or she functions in familiar surroundings, and plan appropriate interventions to enhance physical and psychosocial functioning.

The Elderly Person and I.R.S.

Getting to know an elderly person's uniqueness is the essential element in any therapeutic interaction. As you talk with the person, find out about past and present "I.R.S." —which does not mean "Internal Revenue Service," but instead the person's Identity, Relatedness, and Security. Answers to questions touching on these factors are helpful in revealing I.R.S.:

Identity
    Who am I?
    How am I special?
    What makes me unique?

54

Relatedness

What are my roots? To whom am I related?

To whom do I go when I need someone?

Who comes to me?

With whom do I like to spend time?

Whom do I phone? How often?

With whom do I correspond? How often?

Do I enjoy doing some things alone?

Security

Where was I born? What do I consider my home town?

In how many places have I lived? How long in each?

Do I really consider my present home really home?

Is my present home safe?

Does it support my changing needs?

What daily routines give my day structure?

What lifelong habits do I enjoy?

What new habits do I enjoy now that I am older?

Facts gleaned from these I.R.S. questions can guide the service provider to an understanding of a person's background, culture, values, strengths, coping strategies, social interaction patterns, and perception of the current situation.

Such active participation by the elderly person—the exploration of past and present I.R.S.—can be the first therapeutic intervention. You, the helping professional, have recognized the fact that this person is the authority on his own life. He knows his past life better than anyone else because he has experienced it; he knows his present situation better than anyone else because he is living it.

Understanding past experiences and present situation will permit more effective assessment (with the help of the older person) of environmental, physical, and psychosocial factors that influence functional abilities in home and community. Subsequently, the older person could also join in planning therapeutic interventions to enhance functioning. I have found the following framework useful for this assessment.

Environmental Changes

Changes in the neighborhood can affect an older person's psychosocial functioning. When an old friend dies or moves away, a person loses a cohort and also a role—that of reciprocal helper. This can result in grief work for the loss, and in feelings of isolation as strangers (perhaps of a different generation or culture) move in. If the corner grocery store closes, a source of socialization closes in addition to the source of easy access to necessary supplies. Increased crime in many neighborhoods makes elderly people fearful about going out even in daytime.

Therapeutic Interventions

1. Explore ways to have the older person meet the new neighbors (some older people do not consider it appropriate to initiate an introduction).
2. Offer a "friendly visitor."
3. Arrange for transportation.
4. Explore alternate routes for outings, and initiate a neighborhood "buddy system" so no one goes out alone.
5. Coordinate outings with police patrol schedules.

A home which was in good condition in a person's middle years may need some repairs and changes to compensate for the declining sensory input and slower responsiveness of later years. However, any such changes must be anticipated with appropriate timing and emotional support. To be able to accept the need for changes in the home, the person must first be able to recognize his own declining abilities.

Therapeutic Interventions

1. Repair any raised sidewalks, loose steps, or handrails.
2. Outline steps with contrasting color to increase visibility.
3. Repair screens, door locks, and broken windows.
4. Replace worn electrical cords.
5. Reinforce unstable furniture.
6. Apply non-skid tape to anchor rugs.
7. Provide adequate lighting, especially night lights (the

elderly need three times as much light as persons in their twenties).

8. Place non-skid strips or mats in bath and shower.
9. Install grip bars by shower, bath, and toilet.
10. Check functioning of heaters, stove, and refrigerator; call utility company for necessary repairs.
11. Place a can of baking soda by the stove to be used to extinguish fire.
12. Post emergency numbers near the telephone, using a black felt-tipped pen and large letters to insure visibility.

Physical Changes

General health and physical capabilities of the elderly person strongly influence the ability to function in home and community. Since it is impossible to separate physical and psychological functioning, the following points are significant and should be covered when assessing physical capabilities:

1. Does the elderly person have a current doctor, and has a physical examination been done within the past year? A physical examination is the only way to:
   a. Differentiate between normal and pathological aging.
   b. Assess physical changes which may be affecting behavior.
   c. Re-evaluate effects of medications on the person.
   d. Check out prosthetic devices such as dentures, glasses, and hearing aids and their adequacy for present needs.
2. In relation to personal care, can the elderly person
   a. Attend to daily grooming, including toenails? (These can be a source of infection and subsequent limited mobility.)
   b. Move around the room, up and down stairs, drive a car, use public transportation?
   c. Do personal shopping; prepare properly balanced meals or special diets?

      d. Do routine household tasks in an appropriate length of time?
3. Has the elderly person experienced a recent change in body such as a mastectomy, amputation, or colostomy? Is he recovering from a recent stroke which affects functioning? (These changes—loss of a body part or function—involve the grief process, as well as withdrawal from social function because of feeling "different," inadequate, or rejected.)

Therapeutic Interventions

1. Encourage the older person who has not had a physical to do so; if necessary, help make the appointment with the doctor or an Ambulatory Care Center; arrange transportation and a "supportive other" to accompany the person.
2. Assist in initiating needed, appropriate community resources—visiting nurse service, homemaker help, transportation, food stamps, Meals on Wheels, S.S.I., or legal aid.
3. Encourage involvement in rehabilitation programs and support groups such as those sponsored by the American Cancer Society and the Heart Association.
4. Focus on previous successful coping patterns and strengths.

If a person can be helped to make an optimum "fit" of basic environmental and physical needs with available services, he may be able to experience a renewed interest in his psychosocial needs.

Psychosocial Changes

Inevitably, the elderly person experiences losses in interpersonal relationships and roles. Losses of "significant others" include family, friends, neighbors, and pets. Of all losses, the most stressful can be loss of a peer confidant; the confidant relationship has offered security, protection, caring, understanding, and flexibility through a period of changing functional abilities for both. In addition, the loss of work and work-related roles contribute to feelings of powerlessness and low self-esteem. Such losses can change a person's continuity of life style and daily routines.

In assessing the psychosocial dynamics in an elderly person's life, both changes and continuities need to be considered:

1. The loss of a "significant other" or a role needs to be carefully assessed in relation to the impact on the person's life. Not all losses are negative; some may be perceived by the person to be positive, and some produce ambiguous feelings.
2. The meaning of current relationships must be evaluated:
   a. The family's proximity, frequency of contacts, and exchange of services.
   b. Proximity of friends and neighbors; frequency and contacts and exchange of services.
   c. The significance of pets.
   d. The significance of current social and religious activities.
3. Differentiate between "loneliness" and "being alone."
   a. A person can be alone without being lonely, just as he can be with family, friends, or in a group and experience loneliness.
   b. Feelings of loneliness can be triggered by pain and illness because it is "within oneself"; by loss or lack of relatedness to others, lack of security in a new environment; by inactivity caused by the absence of meaningful plans, nothing to do, no status in a world of the "productive" middle generation.
4. Watch out for "bereavement overload," because the elderly can experience multiple and cumulative losses in a relatively short time. On anniversary dates which focus on a significant loss, special support is needed.

Therapeutic Interventions

Therapeutic interventions which can compensate for social changes should include both family and community resources.
1. Work with the older person to strengthen family ties, if indicated and appropriate, can be most beneficial.
    a. All generations of a family share a common heritage. If the senior family member is given the role of "Family Historian," two desirable results can be achieved. First, such a role can stimulate memories and give the older person an opportunity to do his "life review"—to develop significance and meaning for his life. Secondly, the Family Historian can initiate sharing sessions, in person or by correspondence, to provide a sense of belonging and "roots" for all family members. Sharing of old pictures from the family photo album is an example.
    b. In some cases the family may not be aware of the problems of changes: the elderly person may not have shared this information; he didn't want to be a burden," or was denying the problems himself. Most families are willing to help as much as they can. The service provider can be helpful in working with them to assess realistically if there is a difference between what they would *like* to do and what they *can* do. By supplementing family care with community support services, family members will be able to enjoy "being with" rather than always "doing for" their senior member.
2. Resources in the community can be utilized to help the older person adjust to changing relationships and roles. Peer group affiliations can provide a safe milieu where a person can both build on areas of competence and accept the challenge of new roles. Such resources include the Retired Senior Volunteer Program, Volunteers of America, Gray Panthers, Foster Grandparent Program, American Association of Retired Persons, and the National Association of Retired Teachers.

Summary

Working with the older person to enhance his physical and psychosocial functioning can be mutually challenging and satisfying. I have devised a Check Sheet to help plan appropriate, individualized therapeutic interventions. I hope this tool will be useful as you work with your older people to further develop their Identity, Relatedness, and Security.

Services for the Needy Aged   Check ✓

Basic Services
1. Housing
2. Financial Assistance: Social Security, S.S.I., Medicare, MediCal
3. Out-patient Medical Care, including dental care, eye examination, hearing test, regular physical examination, diagnostic screening tests
4. Mental Health Services
   a. Evaluation
   b. Counseling
5. Nutrition—Food Stamps

Adjustment and Integrative Services
1. Consumer Protection; Legal Aid
2. Information and Referral Service
3. Retirement Counseling
4. Adult Day Care Center: Discussion groups, group meals, podiatrist, barber, beautician, library, classes, day trips
5. Senior Citizen Center
6. R.S.V.P.
7. Gray Panthers
8. Volunteers of America
9. Foster Grandparent
10. A.A.R.P./N.R.T.A.

Supportive Services
1. Home-Help Services
   a. Homemaker Service: Light housekeeping, run errands, do shopping, provide escort service
   b. Household Handyman: Household repair, seasonal tasks including changing screens, yard work, moving furniture
2. Home calls by doctor for evaluation and diagnosis
3. Visiting Nurse Service
4. Rehabilitation—American Cancer Society, Heart Association
5. Friendly Visitor
6. Daily Telephone Reassurance Service
7. Meals on Wheels
8. Home Delivery: Groceries, medicines
9. Transportation
   a. Regular: To clinic, church, day care center
   b. On request
10. Mobile Library Unit
11. Mobile Arts and Craft Unit

Congregate Care Service
1. Adult Foster Care
2. Adult Day Hospital: Day care plus physical therapy, treatment for chronic illnesses, skilled nursing care, dental services

Protective Service
1. Public Gardianship/Conservatorship

Nursing and the Psychosocial Care of the Institutionalized Aged 10

Irene Mortenson Burnside, R.N., M.S.

I would like to share with you five specific concepts I think nursing as a profession, and we as individuals, need to develop more fully if we are going to be instrumental in increasing and upgrading the psychosocial care of the aged.

I'm going to use the word AGING as a memory device. The five letters in aging stand for these five concepts:

> A = Advocacy
> G = Gentleness
> I = Interdisciplinary
> N = Nursing Skills
> G = Goals

A=Advocacy. As nurses we need to be advocates of the aged. The word advocate, even though it is a very fashionable word this year, is still a good one. People who are in distress, in crises, or who are affected with either acute or chronic illnesses all need advocates and seem to require advocacy support. Too often old people are ignored and it is they who really need advocates. Many old people often have few relatives or friends left who could be their advocate.

Those of us who are interested in the aged often have more influence than we realize. Simply having this interest and concern about the aged can rub off on others in unexpected ways. For example, my 20-year-old daughter had to do a class project for a college class on communication. Each week she interviewed an 85-year-old blind man in a nursing home because she said, "Gee, you've got such a cool gerontology library; why shouldn't I use it? It's so handy. It'll save a lot of trips to the library." Needless to say, the old man was terribly pleased especially when she returned after the quarter was over and read the paper to him.

In a working situation nurses are role models for many of the other staff and for student nurses assigned to units for clinical experience. One criticism from instructors who do not want to place students in extended care facilities is the lack of role model nurses in many such agencies. In January of 1969 there were over one million nursing home beds. This should make us aware of the acute need for nurses in this area.[1]

So one important need that must be met by us, both as individuals and as a profession, is the development of a strong advocacy principle. We must advocate for all the aged. We must advocate for those in out-patient clinics, for those in nursing homes, and even for that old lady next door to you who is trying fiercely to stay in her home and maintain her independence.

G = Gentleness. The first "G" in aging stands for gentleness. We are talking about psychosocial care of the aged today. Gentleness is terribly important in this area of care and in the physical care of the aged, too. If you've ever witnessed old people being handled roughly, you'll know what I mean. No wonder they often complain. Many are frail, weak, and in pain. People often rush them, and often not very gently.

Shakespeare said, "Your gentleness shall force, more than your force, move us to gentleness." The wisdom of this sentence is especially apparent in clinical work with the aged. I can think of no other trait needed so much by care givers when they deal with the grieving aged.

I = Interdisciplinary. The "I" in aging stands for Interdisciplinary. I would say that a good example of this concept is here at this workshop. We have an anthropologist, a social worker, two psychiatrists, a physiologist, an architect, and a nurse sharing their views. But as I think about the "I" more, it could also stand for "Invisible." As nurses we are invisible at times. For example, look at interdisciplinary committees. Is there a nurse on the committee? Look at panels. Are there nurses on them? A recent workshop on aging in the Bay Area was co-sponsored by a school of nursing. Nowhere on the program did I see a nurse included.

One rarely finds nurses represented in print. In a book I am reading, a collection of papers entitled *Psychiatric Nursing,* there is one part in the book about understanding the aged patient. Of the nine papers in that section, only two are by nurses and those nurses were not psychiatric nurses! One was in neurology, and one was a public health coordinator. Moore, Tuchin, and Birren have published a bibliography list of 737 dissertations which deal with the aged.[2] Only one was by a nurse.

To improve the psychosocial care of the aged nurses need to be both seen and heard. We need to share our thoughts and ideas and observations with other disciplines. Working with the aged can be a lonely business. I have repeatedly heard nurses say this. We could mitigate some of our professional bereftness and loneliness if we were to mingle with other professionals; become involved in workshops, projects, research, and classes.

N = Nursing Skills. The "N" in aging is for nursing skills. This is an area demanding most of our attention today, so I emphasize it here. Nursing skills is a broad term, so let me make clear what I am not talking about today when I use the phrase "nursing skills." I am not talking about clean beds all lined up in a row, or bedside stands that are cleaned with fervor each week, or patients who are scrubbed until they yell. I am talking about the nursing skills involved in psychosocial nursing care of the elderly.

Today there is a common myth that it doesn't take much nursing skill to work with the aged. (This myth, by the way, has been disproved by a study in England which revealed the level of skilled nursing required for the aged patient.)[3] Within our own profession we have relegated the nurse in the nursing home to a second class citizenry. If you tell someone you work with the aged I am sure you have heard such remarks as, "That must be dull," or "How depressing," or "How do you stand it?" We need to improve the image of the nurse who is interested in the aged.

The typical day of a nurse working within a nursing home setting or on an acute setting where there are many elderly patients is quite revealing. One of my students kept a diary of one of her typical days on a 33 bed unit. Out of 33 patients, 22 were over 65 and six were comatose. I was exhausted when I read her account.

There are many situations demanding psychosocial nursing skill. How do you intervene when an 86-year-old man has just lost his wife of 52 years? He had nursed her tenderly for two years while she suffered from cancer and now he, himself, has a colostomy. Furthermore, he is trying to learn to care for the colostomy himself since his perfectionist daughter-in-law is upset with the mess.

What do you tell waiting relatives when you call a doctor and are told that the doctor cannot come to the convalescent hospital (that's a euphemism, isn't it?) to see their dying mother whom they obviously love deeply? How do you organize nursing care for an elderly patient with an acute illness, or a chronic illness, and a few mental problems thrown in? Add to this the relatives who are hounding you constantly and marking the pads under the patient with a felt-tipped pen to see if you are changing him often enough?

The demands are indeed great on nurses in charge of nursing homes, convalescent hospitals, and wards with a high proportion of elderly patients. Nurses have requested help from me in the psychosocial care of the elderly about the following issues:

1. Grief and bereavement
2. The dying patient
3. Crisis intervention
4. Aphasia
5. Changed body image
6. Confused patients
7. Loneliness
8. Depressions

9. Multiple losses experienced by the aged
10. Sexuality of the aged individual
11. Communication with the elderly

Communication with the aged can often be so difficult that we either ignore its importance or we just give up. Yet, if we want to keep patients in touch with reality, we must communicate with them. Sometimes we don't ask very much of an old person's mind. By failing to do so we reinforce for them the negative views that society has already heaped on them. We must never discount the importance of reminiscence as an important kind of communication for the aged.

When we discuss nursing skills, have we considered and reconsidered (to use one of Dr. Brown's phrases) the nursing rituals and rites we perpetuate? We need to ask the patient what is important to him. Our own value systems get in the way. I'm reminded of the time I tried to convince an old man that aureomycin was more important than snuff. To him, it was not!

Passing medicine is one of our rituals. In one nursing home in Minnesota the elderly patients were in the quiet chapel at the end of the hall praying. It was 8 a.m. and time for 8 a.m. medications. The nurse took the tray of medicines and went into the chapel and passed the medications to the praying people.

Following orders is one of our traditional rituals even if doing so is not in the best interests of the patients. A man was dying of cancer. He was thin, debilitated, and terribly tired. The order for him read, "Be up in chair." Against his wishes, he was bathed and put in a chair; wheeled into the day room to watch TV because "It would be good for him." When his sister visited that night he cried as he told her about his tiring day. The next day he died.

Use of hospital equipment is another ritual area. Consider an ailing elderly couple admitted together to a nursing home or hospital. Where do you get a double bed in an institution? What have we as nurses done to change this? We continue to put people who have slept together for 50 years in separate beds. Sometimes we even put them in separate rooms and often on separate wards. You who are night nurses can tell us some of the results. One nurse I know admitted an elderly couple on the evening shift. She shoved the two single beds together so they could at least reach out and touch one another. She deplored the fact that she could not locate a double bed for them. Such action means, of course, that we have to take a long hard look at our own views about sex in the elderly.

If we did more clinical research, we would know better what rituals and rites to toss out. I have mentioned the importance we attach to pills and medications. People who have been treated with such things as kerosene gargles, mustard plasters, turpentine stupes, and salt pork for wounds aren't much impressed with our long fancy names for pills, our psychedelic-colored ones, or our pills too big for them to swallow. What is important to the aged patient should be our constant question. How often is the patient asked what he needs or wants?

G = Goals. The last letter in aging, the "G," stands for goals. I think as individual nurses we need to delineate realistic goals for ourselves as we care for the aged. I truly believe that at times we need to put on blinders so that we don't see all of the many problems at once. This can be overwhelming. Goals may be quite personal and deal with such things as our own aging or our inability to discuss sex or death. Goals may deal with our own depressions about some of the care we see, or our attempts to formulate a better theoretical base from which to operate.

We need to discover where our expertise lies and capitalize on it. Some of us may excel in the care of the dying patients. Some of us may know how to get crafts sessions or social hours started. Some of us may handle confused, delirious patients well. Some of us may be excellent in administration. This is all a part of knowing ourselves better, and assessing our aptitudes more accurately. Perhaps even realizing that we cannot be all things to all old people would be a good beginning.

One goal I hope we all have is to look carefully at our own nursing care of the aged. This careful look should involve asking questions. Why and how and when is such care different from the nursing care of other groups? Why am I doing this? Is it even necessary? Is there something more therapeutic I can do? The importance of looking at the other side of the coin came home loudly and clearly to me last year when I was interviewing an 80-year-old lady in a nursing home for a research project. She and the aide had a discussion about her siderails, and when the aide left the room, the patient looked me straight in the eye and said, "You think those things are to keep me from falling out of bed, don't you?" I asked cautiously, "Well, what are they really for?" She said, "Well, you would be surprised how many people they keep out of my bed at night!" I have never once thought of that reason for bedrails being up. Have you? That's a good example of what I mean about looking at things differently. Also, let's begin to listen to what the aged patient says about nursing care.

As nurses we need to become involved in research or support research being conducted on our units. Even when a research project is not a five-year, grant-funded project, it still is important. The very activity of researchers on a ward is beneficial, as I see it, to both staff and patients. I am reminded of a little old lady who came to a nursing station and said, "Is Herbert Hoover or Lyndon Johnson president of the United States?" The nurse gave her the correct answer; then cautiously asked the sweet, little, confused lady why she wanted to know. She answered, "Well, there is this nice young man here on the ward, and every day he goes around asking who is President of the United States, and I just thought I would like to help him."

There are many possibilities for research with the aged. We need to look at the differences between the young old, the middle-aged old, and the very old. For example, are there more centenarians around these days? How many of you have spent time with 100-year-old patients? What are they like? There are few controlled studies on group work (done by any discipline, not to mention nurses) with the aged population. We know that suicide rates in the elderly men are high, and are usually preceded by a depression. Nursing research could be done in the area of depression and suicide in the aged.

How does the disengagement theory fit into nursing care?

The constriction of space that the elderly experience is another area for research. Think about space or privacy in a three-bed, crowded ward that is your permanent home.

Marjorie Lowenthal suggests that a confidant relationship helps a person survive the loss of a spouse. Do elderly patients develop a confidant relationship with a nurse? Can nurses become pseudo-families? What's been tried by nurses in the way of family therapy with the aged?

How can we (or do we) encourage reminiscing by the aged patient? We tend to cut them off, fearing the memories will be painful for them. Dr. Brown talked about "the need for the continuity of life experience." There is certainly research to be done by nurses in this important area in gerontology.

If nothing else we surely can begin to utilize the research which has already been done. Goffman and Caudill have studied institutions. What would it be like to be admitted to a nursing home for a day or two and experience its odors and sounds and sights? What about decision-making and the aged? What about staff control in these "controlled environments"? What about the ways the aged patients control and manipulate nurses? How many studies are there by nurses on the dying aged patient? Studies reported at gerontology conferences are done by social workers or psychologists. Have we looked at the dying rituals with the aged patient in institutions? What are the effects on patients and staff when funerals are held in the nursing homes? These research goals are within our reach.

There are other possible goals. To articulate increasingly our beliefs. To be more visible. To dare to be innovative instead of always routine. To try better to understand what it might be like to be 80 or 90 or 100 years old by listening attentively to old people. Dr. Brown talks about resensitizing ourselves. This is one way to begin. To consider our attitudes about sexuality and death in the aged. To strive for individuality in ourselves, and to promote it in our aged patients. A French author says: "To think and act as an individual is still one of the best ways of postponing the onset of incurable senility."[4]

Florida Scott-Maxwell has said it beautifully: "Old people can seldom say 'we'. Not those who live alone. Even those who live with their families are alone in their experience of age. So the habit of thinking in terms of 'we' goes, and they become 'I'. It takes increasing courage to be 'I' as one's frailty increases."[5] This is the goal I would like to end with. The goal for each of us: to encourage the aged to maintain his or her "I" no matter how frail he or she may become.

"Aging" is a word I have tried to use with care by using the individual letters in the word. Aging can mean advocacy, gentleness, interdisciplinary, nursing skills, and new goals for all of us, as we move together to increase and change the nurses' role in the psychosocial care of the aged.

[1]Nursing homes beds top a million. *American Journal of Nursing,* 1969, *69*(10), 2000.
[2]Moore, J. L., Tuchin, M. S., & Birren, J. E. A bibliography of doctoral dissertations on aging from American institutions of higher learning, 1934-1969. *Journal of Gerontology,* 1971, *26*(3), 391-442.
[3]Irvine, R. E., & Smith, B. J. Geriatric care demands highest quality nursing. *Geriatric Focus,* 1970, *9*(5), 1.
[4]Guillerme, J. *Longevity.* New York: Walker & Co., 1963. (p. 130)
[5]Scott-Maxwell, F. *The measure of my days.* New York: Alfred A. Knopf, 1969. (pp. 130-131)

11 Utilizing the Health Team in the Care of the Aged

Elsie A. Giorgi, M.D.

For too long we have been reciting a litany of the dismal future of our health services. Finally we are making some progress. At least there is now general acknowledgement that the American Way of Health is chaotic, that our health care delivery system is truly sick and disorganized, and that we are ready for a change in therapy. However, with this comes the fear that the medical profession, supposedly central to the delivery of care, may well be too sick itself to effect a cure or to help heal a sick society. Instead of being a prophet of doom and gloom, I would like to discuss with you some solutions I feel would be reasonable, achievable, and effective.

An Effective Health Care Delivery System

An effective health care delivery system must be comprehensive. It must address the total health care needs of people and also provide for the total population. We can immediately define three types of "patients"—the individual, the family, and the community—as units demanding care. If recovery means providing significant health care, all three of these patients are "more troubled than sick." The term "medical care" must be discarded for the concept of "health care." Medical care is only a small part of what people, families, and communities need in terms of care. The services we render must be preventive and restorative, as well as curative. They must address psychosocial as well as biological needs. They must be comprehensive, coordinated, and continuing as well as available, accessible, and acceptable.

This immediately implies that no physician and no single health profession can possibly go it alone. A multidisciplinary team approach is required. Tasks must be completed by trained para- and non-professionals, especially by peers of the group receiving care. Health agents, peer-related generalists and specialists, and informed patients' advocates must be given more than lip service if we are to overcome manpower shortages and patient resistances. We must decentralize our monstrous medical ghettoes, our urban public hospitals, so we can bring services to the indigent. Otherwise we have to continue to ignore the fact that these people either cannot get to us or they avoid coming until it "hurts too much" to stay away.

We must stop talking about "medicine for the poor." Poverty characterizes less than 12% of our population. We seem to have a great need these days to romanticize poverty and discrimination. Our entire population is badly in need of quality care at reasonable cost.

We must stop our piecemeal approach to care which can offer only fragmented, overlapping, duplicated, and often depersonalized services. For the most part, the sick are buying professional "time," not "care." Time and care are very different entities.

In order to accomplish this, two very important concepts must be addressed. These are two considerations which will be important as we work toward the goal of comprehensive health care. First, levels of care must be based on levels of need. The recipient of care (the patient) and not the provider must be central in all planning. Second, the Right Patient must be treated in the Right Place at the Right Time under the Right Supervision based on his needs at any single time. This requires that all modalities of care be available as needed. There must be free transfer between them as soon as maximum benefit is reached through any single one. This is true continuing care with an ongoing treatment and referral plan. This plan must be a collaborative effort involving the basic team—physician, nurse, and social worker.

In acute illness, the physician will lead the team. In subacute, the nurse will lead, and in chronic illness, it will be the social worker who will lead. Why not? Depending upon the patient's condition, the members of the basic team may be acting as leaders or consultants.

The health agent can become a very active coordinating generalist, picking up the slack by performing those chores which do not require professional skill. Most are chores which are now being done by us so that scarce professional time is being wasted. The health agent can more easily overcome the barrier of professionalism which is often confusing to and even distrusted by our patients and clients.

Experiences With The Health Care Team

The Health Team Concept is glibly bantered about these days. We talk a great deal and conceptualize a great deal. But we do precious little. We are still very far from a true delineation of roles, from a true understanding of the concept, and, most important of all, from a realistic approach to implementation.

I would like to share with you some of my own thoughts on meaning and implementation. My very first experience goes far back to my training days at Bellevue when all I knew of the nurse was that she constantly nagged us to get our work done. We thought the whole idea of our internship and residency was for learning rather than serving. The patient was less important than our educational and research needs. The social worker was thought of as someone who would "get rid of" the patient for us when he was no longer interesting. We didn't care where the patient went after we were through with him. We ranted and raved if the social worker didn't get him out of our way in a hurry. We were quite a non-team. No wonder so many of our patients bounced right back to us. There was no concept of continuing care.

There were some good things that happened at Bellevue though, too. I got my first glimpse at the effects of chronic illness on people and I learned about the team approach to care management. In trying to get rid of patients on the ward, we suddenly had home care problems.

Next there was an unforgettable experience in East Harlem, New York. There was a neighborhood health center there. It was located in a small apartment on East 100th Street. This block is often referred to as the worst block in New York. It was. There I first learned about the total health concept and about the true value of the public health nurse, the community-based social worker, and the peer-related community worker. We watched a dismal, degraded community come to life. Neighborhood health centers really got started there. There were three doctors involved in the project and we used to come on different days. I found myself going to the neighborhood center more than to my office. I was so excited over what was happening there.

Within two years after working in East Harlem, I got to make use of all that wonderful experience. We initiated our programs of continuing care, extended care, and home health care at Cedars-Sinai Medical Center. The entire program revolved around a very effective and meaningful health team approach. The team consisted of three physicians plus me. There were also two social workers, a liaison Public Health Nurse, a physical therapist, and an occupational therapist. That was coordinated home care, and not what we have today. We had all sorts of medical and surgical sub-specialists, dentists, and a full range of paramedical workers, all for $8.45 a day. We used the VNA Public Health Nurse for home visits.

The patients were staffed once a week in a three hour session. The situation at Cedars-Sinai is ideal for a team approach. There are very complete resources. There are facilities, equipment and manpower available most of the time. We can program the patient's needs in the framework of continuing care, treating the right patient at the right place at the right time. We have at Cedars-Sinai ambulatory care, acute hospital care, chronic disease care, and a geriatric day center which we call the Nelton Garden. This is where we really share our powers in therapy, rather than leaving the power with the doctor.

What happened at Cedars-Sinai was a very wonderful experience for all of us. The roles were dictated not so much by discipline, but by patient need. It wasn't unusual for the nurse, for example, to make a clinical diagnosis and recommendation.

There was never any feeling among us of others encroaching on our professional territory. The patients (and not ourselves) were central to therapy. We also made the best use of available services at all times. We used established community services whenever possible and eliminated duplicated services. And there was a central control over the project through our staffing conferences. Later, when we began to expand into a private patient care, we made use of the conference telephone in order to involve the private physician. This was the idea of our chief social worker, Ceil Mittelman. The nurse/social worker part of the team was very active in recruitment of patients. These people went into the wards. They evaluated patients practically at time of their admission and recommended to the physician a continuing care program for the patient. Their recommendations were extremely well accepted. When this system was discontinued because of hospital priorities (a new building rather than new programs) many physicians called me and bemoaned the absence of this team which had been so helpful to them. If you wish to learn more about this program, I would suggest that you send for the H.E.W./P.H.S. film entitled, "Medicine at the Crossroads."

Next there was the O.E.O./Watts Health Center. We had much difficulty implementing the Health Team there because of physicians' resistance. However, it is off the ground at present and is much like the program at Cedars-Sinai.

I was next involved in a program of Comprehensive Care at the Orange County Medical Center. This program also makes the fullest use of the Health Team Concept. We have recently added the health educator and nutritionist to the team. We are moving towards the concept of a Health Protection Center with a Multiphase Screening/Comprehensive

Care Clinic at its hub. H.E.W. is becoming very interested in this program as a possible prototype for other urban public hospitals (the horrible medical ghettoes) so badly in need of reorganization.

Very briefly, this is how the program operates: we have reorganized the Emergency Room, the point of entry for the patient into our Health Care System. Next, we select our patients for the Comprehensive Care Clinic. The criteria for selection involves the identification of patients with (1) some promise of looking on our hospital as the chief source of their care and (2) those with multiple problems, either biological or psychosocial or both. After the interval (episodic) illness is improved, the patient goes through our Multiphasic Screening Program. As he goes through, health agents assist him to understand the program and to complete the total health questionnaire. Then the Public Health Nurse and Social Worker scan the biographical information and begin to match patient needs with the available services. After all reports are available, the team meets to discuss a multidisciplinary approach to the patient's problems. The team makes full use of community units, facilities, and organizations to do this. The health educator and nutritionist will be used as consultants to the team. They will also be used for preparation of instructional materials for staff and patients.

Finally the patient is referred to the Comprehensive Care Clinic where he is examined by the interns to whom he is assigned. An attending physician, the house staff member, and the paramedical team then discuss the patient again towards the goal of meeting his needs. We are also conducting an ongoing health agent training program for non-professionals, using volunteers as well as employees. Every clerk is being taught to be an informed patient advocate.

Basic Requirements for an Effective Health Care Team

Implementing the Health Care Team requires not only the team members or the concept, but also the services needed for comprehensive care. This does not necessitate a hospital base. A free-standing unit can also do well provided it has access to all the required components. Preferably, such access should be through meaningful and firm affiliation. A clinic could do it as well as a V.N.A. agency or a public health unit. The requirements are simply coordination and meaningful affiliation.

It is necessary for the team concept to be accepted by professionals. No doubt there will be resistance. It is a resistance which evolves chiefly from ignorance. Of course, patients are an essential part of the program. You will be frustrated, but I hope you will not be discouraged. Don't forget that you have something valuable to offer. At the Orange County Medical Center, we met with resistances, but the physicians and the administration quickly noted the improvement in services and the lowered overall costs through meaningful coordination. The interns, the teaching-supervisory community, and the faculty physicians like the program because it puts them back into doctoring. Incidentally, doctors are seeing twice as many patients. The new patient census has doubled while the comeback visits have decreased by at least half. The community public health nurse liaison and social work group therapy have also helped considerably. Our patients are indeed "more troubled than sick." We are also analyzing the change in the number of medications and tests ordered. A preliminary evaluation indicates that this has improved also.

Soon we hope to have an Extended and Home Health Care Program and a detoxification unit for alcohol and drug ingestion. Our goal is to create a Department of Continuing Care and Community Health. This will be a backstop for community physicians, permitting them to order the needed medical and psychosocial services for their patients. This will let doctors provide comprehensive care in their offices by the writing of a simple order. Doctors are impatient for this to happen. The Health Team will organize and energize the whole program. Patients will get the care they really need rather than the patchwork, fragmented, and depersonalized care they previously received. It should be apparent that the Health Team can become the means to coordinate and unify our Health Care Delivery System towards creating a Biomedical Complex. This is essential if we are to properly care for our people and if we are to render complete and quality care at reasonable cost. I think the Health Care Team could well become the main focus of Health Care in the future. It could solve a good many of our current problems provoked by an exceedingly poor, almost irrelevant, and very costly Health Care Delivery System.

At the same time, I don't want to leave the impression that it is either simple or clear sailing. We still have much to do, and we could get stopped at any moment, especially as the result of Medi-Cal cutbacks. But if we worried about the failures, we would never try. I am always encouraged by something my high school coach once said to me when I was learning to be a hurdle jumper. She said, "Don't look at the hurdles; look at the goal!" These words offer a philosophy which has universal applicability. It helps to remember it.

Standards for Geriatric Nursing Care: The Where, Who, How, Why, What, and When of It

12

Lois N. Knowles, R.N., M.A.

The development of standards in the field of geriatric nursing is important for the individual nurse and the entire nursing profession. When standards are presented, these are some of the questions that are sure to be raised immediately: From where and from whom do standards come? How do standards become a part of nursing practice and how can they be recognized in practice? Why do geriatric nurses want standards? Why do geriatric nurses need standards? What is a standard? What are some problems in measuring how a standard is being met? What are some ways to measure the quality of nursing? What method of measurement has been chosen by your Standards Committee? When should standards be used? This discussion responds to these questions.

Where, Who, and How?

From where and from whom do standards for nursing come? How can standards be put into practice and how can they be recognized?

At some time all good nurses need a list of standards for nursing practice. The nurse believes that if she follows her list of standards for nursing practice the result will be a high quality of nursing. To put it another way, the nurse believes that her actions will positively affect the well-being of the individual patient. Nurses need to have a list of standards for nursing care actions, and they need to know how to measure their effectiveness as helping people. Establishing standard practices means we believe that the patient will be better off because of these nursing actions than without them.

Nurses try to raise the level of a patient's "wellness" as high as possible. They must also be able to recognize when "wellness" cannot be the goal, and subsequently to assist the patient at declining levels and ultimately with death.

Every nurse has a set of standards that she uses in her nursing practice. Up until October 1969 these standards (which would help to identify adequate, good, or superior standards of geriatric nursing practice) existed only in our heads and never on paper. Recognition that these implicit standards do exist can be implied from: (1) reports communicating nursing actions from one shift to the next; (2) nursing care plans illustrating the nurse's thoughtful consideration of patient needs in written form; (3) research studies reporting the effects of certain nursing action on patients; (4) various professional journal articles focusing on specific aspects of nursing; and (5) case studies and other information sources.

Published lists of items nurses consider important in nursing care have been few and far between. I have worked with Mrs. Rowena Rogers on a report about nursing actions and the frequency of their need. The nursing problems were identified from the patient's nursing history. Next Mrs. Rogers listed the appropriate nursing order to respond to the need. Each nursing action has a goal. A standard is this goal which relates to each nursing action.

An example follows of a nursing plan for a female patient who was admitted to a nursing home with problems of incontinency, feelings of uselessness and low self-esteem, apparent apathy and depression. Although she could walk, she had not walked during the four weeks she had been home from the hospital. This lady's deafness had been corrected with a hearing aid. She was beginning to withdraw and disengage herself from the world around her. With this history, the following nursing plan was outlined for this woman.

Nursing Plan

Nursing Problems	Nursing Orders or Actions	Frequency	Most Related Standard(s) of Geriatric Nursing[1]
Incontinent of urine and feces	Bowel and Bladder Continency Routine		Standard No. 4. The nurse supports & promotes normal physiological functioning of the older person.
	1. Help her to bathroom q 1 h waking hours q 2 h sleeping hours	9:00 10:00, 11:00, etc. 11:00 p.m., 1:00 3:00, 5:00, 7:00	
	2. Verbally acknowledge successes; ignore failures		
	3. Administer prescribed suppository q.d.	9:30 a.m.	
	4. Prune juice or prunes q.d. at breakfast	8:00	
	5. Inspect skin around perineum q.d.	9:00	
	6. To wear underwear and street clothes q.d.	9:00	

[1] *American Nurses' Association, Division on Geriatric Nursing Practice, Draft Copy of Standards for Geriatric Nursing Practice, March 23, 1970, 10 Columbus Circle, New York, N.Y. 10019.*

Nursing Problems	Nursing Orders or Actions	Frequency	Most Related Standard(s) of Geriatric Nursing
Patient feels useless (her words) Has low self esteem Seems apathetic and depressed	To attend remotivation session q.d. 1. To bring her own handmade quilt to Thursday session (topic: quilts) 2. To wear perineal pad to remotivation session and to meals only; these are to be removed immediately after these events.	10:15-10:45 a.m.	Standard No. 3. The nurse demonstrates an appreciation of the heritage, values, and wisdom of older persons. Standard No. 6. The nurse employs a variety of methods to promote effective communication and social interaction of aged persons with individuals, family, and other groups.
Immobility; can walk but has not done so for four weeks	Orders for continency routine and remotivation sessions will be used for this problem.		Standard No. 7. The nurse together with the older person designs, changes, or adapts physical and psychosocial environment to meet his needs within the limitations imposed by the situation.
Deafness	Make mechanical check on hearing aid 1. Replace batteries q.d. on odd numbered days. 2. Check parts q.d. 3. Daughter is to bring batteries weekly Talk with her, using nursing orders for deafness routine and how to adjust to wearing a hearing aid. (refer to procedure book.)	3:00 p.m.-10/23 10/25; 10/27; 10/29 3:00 p.m. Tuesdays 3:00 p.m.	Standard No. 8. The nurse assists older persons to obtain and utilize devices which help them to attain a higher level of function, and ensures that these devices are kept in good working order by the appropriate persons or agencies.

Nursing Plan (Cont'd.)

Nursing Problems	Nursing Orders or Actions	Frequency	Most Related Standard(s) of Geriatric Nursing
Beginning disengagement	Talk with her about her life in Georgia and/or detective stories q.d. at lunch and dinner.	1:00 & 6:00	Standard No. 1. The nurse observes and interprets minimal as well as gross signs and symptoms associated with both normal aging and pathological changes and institutes appropriate nursing measures.
	1. Provide reading materials—detective stories q.d.	9:00	
	2. Do not allow patient's reading to interrupt other nursing orders. (Be prepared for hostile remarks from Mrs. Z when her reading is interrupted.)		
Increased dependency	Encourage her to express her feelings		Standard No. 9. The nurse seeks to resolve her conflicting attitudes regarding aging, death and dependency so that she can assist older persons to maintain life with dignity and comfort until death ensues.
	1. If she is angry, try saying "You are upset . . .".		
	2. If she mentions dying, stay with her and listen for clues to help.		

Nursing progress notes should be kept to indicate how the nursing actions are affecting the behavior or symptoms of the patient.

Notes about this patient's progress would probably read like this:

> Incontinent ten times out of thirteen checks during day and four out of five checks during night. Often states, "I am such a baby; I cannot even go to the bathroom by myself." Nurse has reflected this stated feeling, and once patient cried when she did. Use of touch by patting shoulder seemed to help her to understand that the nurse understood her feelings. Cried one-half hour after this. Attended remotivation session (subject: apples). Seemed to be quite interested, but only spoke once. Needs quite a lot of physical support to get to the bathroom. Is really tired at the end of the day. Says she has not walked this much for three months. Has been sleeping most of the nights except when wakened for continency routine. Skin around perineum is in good condition (pink and with no abrasions). Turns her hearing aid off when she reads. Will not talk about what she reads. Future plans: I will have to start reading Perry Mason so I will know who the characters are so I can talk with her. Needs a better reading light. Could use a magnifying glass or a large print book. New orders entered on chart.

These are some of the standards the Committee on Geriatric Nursing of the American Nurses' Association has established for geriatric nursing. These standards represent those of 800 geriatric nurses from all over the United States. The lists of quality nursing actions which individual nurses have been carrying around in their heads now have been put together and written down. All of the suggestions and recommendations which the geriatric nurses in this country mailed back to the Standards Committee, together with those made at the meeting in Gainesville, were studied by the Committee on Standards of the Division on Geriatric Nursing of the ANA.

To answer the first questions, from where and from whom do standards for geriatric nursing come? They come from geriatric nurses themselves.

How then do these standards become a part of nursing practice? Standards become a part of practice when the nurse takes a nursing history or when she makes an assessment, when she identifies patient problems or when she makes a list of nursing orders and carries these out, when she knows her goals for care, or when she writes patient progress notes. Standards become a part of nursing practice when the nurse knows the theory on which her nursing is based.

Why?

Why do geriatric nurses want standards? Why do geriatric nurses need standards?

The answer is that one of the primary goals of any helping profession is to control the practice and actions of its members to improve the service clients receive.

We need standards desperately so that nurses will be able to identify goals they think are important not only for themselves but for their patients and families, for the general public, and for legislators. If the nursing profession wishes to communicate what it considers quality nursing standards to be, there must be a list of such standards. For our professional survival we must delineate our own professional standards.

A distinction needs to be made between the licensure of practitioners by lawmakers and the self-judgment of nurses of their own profession. Nurses have initiated and brought about legislation in order to evaluate and adequately control nursing practitioners. Naturally the state is interested in protecting people from incapable, deceptive, and fraudulent practitioners. So are nurses. Nursing organizations develop strength through their unified efforts and through established means of professional communication.

One example of effective professional communication is the *American Journal of Nursing.* This journal is a means for exchanging knowledge, techniques, and accomplishments. From its beginnings in 1900, one of the objectives of its publication has been to encourage communication between nurses so that uniform legislation could be secured in all states.

The nursing profession itself has continually conducted surveys and written reports. A Standard Curriculum for the School of Nursing was published by the National League for Nursing Education in 1917. The nursing profession developed

Standards for Enrollment in the American Red Cross, established a National Accreditation Program for Schools of Nursing, developed a National State Board Test Pool, employed Executive Secretaries in State Nurses' Associations to assist with legislation protecting the rights of nurses, creating a Bureau of State Board of Nursing Examiners in 1943 and establishing conferences for State Board representatives of the AMA to consider problems of mutual concern.

State licensure to practice is merely a ticket for admission to the profession. Theoretically, in order to remain in good standing in the profession, a nurse must practice in ways that are acceptable to her peers. The problem is that revocation of licensure to practice has customarily involved only such behavior as drug addiction and alcoholism. These are quite different issues than trying to evaluate the quality of nursing practice being practiced. An alcoholic nurse might be capable of giving excellent nursing care, but her license is revoked on the assumption that alcoholics give poor nursing care. No one knows exactly what poor nursing care means.

Another reason nurses need to identify good nursing standards is so we can improve the quality of our nursing practice. Since nurses have had little experience doing this, we need to consider how other clinical professions judge their members' professional performance.

Consider for example, the medical audit. Hospital records are reviewed against criteria which include qualitative judgment of the care given, diagnostic errors, mortality rates, rates of specific complications, removal of normal tissues at operations, consultations, rates for Caesarean section, and so forth. These are some of the standards used to measure the quality of medical practice.

Because there are no set standards for nursing practice nurses have become alarmed. Nurses feel that they have a responsibility to set forth standards to evaluate the nursing practice. It is thought that this self-appraisal would serve as a stimulus to improve the quality of care. The present agitation in the American Nurses' Association is expected to stimulate an improved quality of practice by nurses themselves, and not to result in state legislation governing standards of the nursing practice. Improvements in the standards of nursing in each of the various clinical-specialty divisions of the American Nurses' Association are particularly expected. In an age of specialization, it seems appropriate that nursing now is about to develop standards for the various specialties of nursing.

There are additional reasons why we need standards for nursing. The "ANA in Action" states that established standards can be used as one criterion for the certification of geriatric nurses. The criteria for certification will be made initially by an Interim Board for each of the five ANA divisions of practice. The purpose is (1) to recognize members who exhibit excellence in practice, and (2) to recognize members for their high level of achievement or for making outstanding contributions to their profession.

Why does an organization such as the ANA want to recognize good practice by its members? The reasons are: (1) "to advance the art and science of the profession," (2) "to protect the public by specifying those members qualified to function in special areas," and (3) "to recognize and award superior performance and leadership."

Other professions that recognize outstanding members follow various procedures for selecting such persons. Some recognize members on the recommendation of peers. Very often the procedure requires that the applicant submit standardized forms to the Certification Board. Applicants submit background material and usually pay a fee. Applicants have usually made an outstanding contribution to their profession. Some professions require various combinations of (1) education, (2) a number of years of practice, and (3) a contribution to the profession. Most other professional organizations also require proof of excellence of practice through (4) evaluation of work submitted (by written and/or oral examination, or by submission of materials and examination). In addition, most consider (5) education beyond that required for general practice, (6) a specified length of time in practice, (7) outstanding contributions, (8) specialized advanced training, (9) membership in the official organization, and (10) active practice in the profession at the time of application. Certification committees use a number to identify outstanding members. Perhaps nursing needs to use a combination of these criteria.

What?

What is a standard? What is a standard for nursing? What are some methods of measuring the quality of nursing? What method has been chosen by the Standards Committee?

Webster defines a standard as something established by authority, custom, or general consent as a model or example. A standard applies to any definite rule, principle, or measure established by authority and it is a measurement of recognized excellence or established authority. One suggested definition for a nursing standard is "an authoritative statement describing certain specifications by which an assessment of nursing practice can be made."

What are some of the problems in measuring the quality of care? Sheps says that the problem in measuring the quality of hospital care is its multidimensional nature. It is a service provided by a coordinated group of professional, technical, and other workers. The quality of that service is affected by the adequacy of facilities and their maintenance, the administrative and professional organization of the hospital, the competence of personnel, and the interpersonal relationships among the staff and between staff and patients.

There are at least six methods of measuring the quality of care:

Measuring the Outcome of Care

Peterson states that the quality of medical care may be measured by the end results. For example, it is possible to count the number of patients who recover or who die from hernia operations. The number of patients who have had complications can be counted. Outcome of care has been used as a measurement of quality in terms of recovery, restoration of function, or survival. But is the outcome of care in fact a measure relevant to what we want to measure? Survival may be a criterion for success even when it is accompanied by suboptimal health or crippling. Factors other than medical may determine outcome. If valid conclusions are to be drawn, these other factors must be held constant.

Measuring by Observation

A second means of measurement is that of directly observing the professional. This method is of limited value because of the problem of sampling, observer bias, and reproductibility (although video tape or film, which could repeat a clinical situation, would assist in reducing the significance of these problems).

Measuring by Reviewing Records

A third means of measurement would be to review records in view of a set of established standards. Donabedian observes, "The assessment of quality must rest on a conceptual and operational definition of what it means." The quality of care, according to Lee and Jones, is presented in the form of eight "articles of faith." Some are stated as attributes or properties of the process of care and others as goals or objectives of the process. They define quality as a reflection of values and goals current in the medical care system and in the larger society of which it is a part. Again, the problem can readily be seen: to hold the other factors constant if valid conclusions are to be drawn.

Measuring the Process of Care

A fourth means of measuring the quality is to examine the process of care itself rather than its outcome. This is the method described by Donabedian as evaluation of the quality of medical care. Is good medical (nursing) care being applied? "Judgements are based on considerations such as appropriateness, completeness, and redundance of information obtained through clinical histories, physical examinations, and diagnostic tests; justification of diagnoses and therapy; technical confidence in the performance of diagnostic and therapeutic procedures, including surgery; evidence in preventive management in health and illess; coordination and continuity of care; acceptability of care to the recipient and so on." Although these estimates of quality are less stable and less final than those which measure outcomes, they may be more relevant to the question at hand—whether care is being properly practiced. This same means of measuring nursing could help to identify, treat and evaluate nursing care for the patient.

Measuring the Nursing Care Setting

Donabedian describes another approach to assessment which involves evaluating the environment setting where the nursing care takes place. This involves the assessment of structures, including administrative support and direct provision of care. Studying settings rather than care itself means looking at the adequacy of facilities and equipment, the qualifications of medical (nursing) staff and their organization, administrative structures and operating programs, fiscal organization, and so on. This approach offers the advantage of fairly concrete and assessable information for measurement. One limitation of this method is that the relationship between the structure, the process of structure, and the outcome is not very well established yet.

Measuring Program Impact

A fifth approach in measuring quality is to study the effect of specific programs or specialized procedures on the quality of care. These would include examining the impact of conferences and regional programs such as the Heart, Cancer and Stroke Centers now being tried experimentally. Do these programs affect the quality of care being given?

We could use any or all of these measurements to evaluate the quality of nursing care. Although the nursing profession has studied the settings in which nursing takes place, the facilities and the number of personnel, it has few studies which directly attempt to measure quality of care. Our history reveals more evaluations of settings than of the nursing practice being conducted within the setting. Recently Medicare has started to require measurements of skilled nursing care by examining the medical orders for the patient. However, there is no plan to measure the nursing practice or to reward quality nursing care other than carrying out the physician's orders for his plan of care. Is the government right in assuming that following the specific medical orders results in good nursing care?

The Standards Committee has developed a list of statements which delineates activities that nurses need to consider in their practice. The statements represent the accumulated knowledge of the geriatric nurses on the Committee. The geriatric nurse membership of the ANA gave the Committee the authority to set these standards. The Committee periodically checks and updates the standards with geriatric nurses throughout the country. This means that the standards represent the general consensus of the membership. The nurse who uses these principles in her nursing practice demonstrates her acceptance of criteria which may be used to measure her nursing practice.

By using or implementing this code of conduct, set of principles, or basic standards, nurses can evaluate quality of nursing care. They can (1) measure the result of their actions on the patient (outcome), (2) observe the practicing of nursing, (3) evaluate the process of care itself (the assessment of planning, implementing and evaluating care), (4) assess the effects of the environment on the patient, and/or (5) assess the result of particular programs on nursing care.

The American Nurses' Association predicts that if the nurse performs certain activities in relation to the standards that quality nursing care will result. We cannot guarantee the effect of all these activities on geriatric patients, but in our judgement if these are performed they produce better nursing than if they are not performed.

What other sources and methods can be used for obtaining information as to how nurses are carrying out their standards?

Clinical records can be examined. The important thing here is to note the logic that governs the nursing activities rather than the absolute validity of the activity itself. In other words, how did the nurse make a decision about what she did? One researcher indicated that an interview helps (in 12.6% of the total number of cases) supplement the written patient record. When what is being said differs from what is on the chart, a great deal of frustration occurs. An interviewer needs to ask herself and the nurse, "What is going on here? Why is there a difference?" The clinical record should reflect both the decision and its reasons.

The nurses' activities can be directly observed by a well

qualified colleague. An overestimate of quality rather than the reverse often results when this method is used. It is difficult for the observer to judge whether the nurse's action is appropriate to the situation at the time or whether the nurse is acting from previous knowledge of the patient.

Nurses could be judged by their peers. What happens when a member of a nurse's family needs nursing care? To which nursing home or hospital or extended care facility would you be willing to send your family member?

What measurement is used depends on the way we define our standards. Standards can come from two sources. The first are empirical standards derived from actual practice and used to compare nursing care in one city (or situation) with that in another. The second are normative standards which are demonstrably attainable levels of care. For this reason they enjoy a certain degree of credibility and acceptance.

In principle, normative standards derive from sources that legitimately set the standards of knowledge and practice in the nursing care system. They are set by standard textbooks, publications, panels of nurses or highly qualified practitioners, or by research staff in coordination with qualified practitioners. "Normative standards can be very high and represent the best care that can be provided or they can be set at a more modest level signifying acceptable, or adequate, care. Their distinctive characteristic is that they stem from a body of legitimate knowledge and values, rather than from specific examples of actual practice. At first, they depend for their further validity on the extent of agreement concerning facts and values within the profession, or at least among its leadership."

One way of measuring is to assign a weight to each item on the list of standards. These weights can be decided by leaders in the profession. The items can then be added up and averaged, yielding an overall assessment value. For example, in medicine particular emphasis is placed on the diagnosis, since appropriate treatment cannot proceed without it. This treatment factor would be more weighed because it is considered more valuable.

The judged effectiveness of care depends on the individual members of society or on the subculture receiving health care. These people are the ultimate judges of the quality of care. The validity of all other measurements standards as indicators of quality depends ultimately on the relationship between the measurements and the attainment of health and the satisfaction of the people receiving care.

The therapy, or what the nurse does in relation to presenting nursing problems (such as those of feeding, dressing, moving, motivating, or communicating with elderly patients) theoretically helps increase the life satisfaction or at least maintains the patient's life style. The achievement of this goal would reflect the adequacy of standards of care in the geriatric nursing programs for the elderly.

When?

Although there is no deadline for completing the statement of ANA standards (necessary for the certification process), matters proceeded in record time for the Standards Committee of the Geriatric Division of the ANA until the financial crisis. With some modifications, the recommended standards have been adopted by the Certification Interim Board. I think you will be pleased to know that the Geriatric Division was the first division to get its standards ready together with an introductory statement and specific examples of the standards. Perhaps because geriatric nursing has been recognized so recently, the members of this committee were particularly concerned to state the ways geriatric nursing differs from other kinds of nursing.

Although the date of certification is indefinite, it need not let us keep from implementing the standards at once. Many of us started a long time ago to improve the standards of geriatric nursing. Many have worked to recognize the outstanding persons in our profession for certification.

Every one of us already has a standard of nursing care for geriatric nursing. What the Standards Committee has done is to write down the standards nurses have had in their heads. I would like the group to know that the standards have been revised four times by the Committee, and that these four revisions were based largely upon the responses of a possible 4,565 nurses who were asked to react to the standards. The Committee has tried to write down the standards that geriatric nurses all over the country have been using to delineate what nurses consider essential to geriatric nursing. Some of these standards are shared standards of practice in all of the different specialties in nursing. These standards will need to change as knowledge changes.

In summary, the reason for establishing standards is to improve the quality of nursing, particularly geriatric nursing practice. Another reason is to identify outstanding practitioners of nursing. All of us would like to be outstanding practitioners of nursing, I believe, and standards should help us toward that goal. These standards will help nurses communicate the ways they have been able to help patients. To recognize nurses who are doing an excellent job in nursing is certainly worthwhile, not only to reward the nurse herself, but also to encourage professional pride and to give patients better care. It should be a relief to nurses that nursing can be evaluated for the quality of its care rather than through a numerical count of the number of beds, the number of people in them, or the number of nurses.

13

The Adult Day Care Center Experience (SHIP, Tucson, Arizona)

Gordon Purdy, M.S.W.

The Senior Health Improvement Programs (SHIP) of Handmaker Jewish Geriatric Center of Tucson, Arizona, is an adult day care program which has been operating continuously since 1967. During its history, this program has served at least 2,000 elderly people.

Formal research has begun only recently. However, our staff has accumulated a great deal of knowledge concerning our participants or clients. This information is the basis for some of our most effective work.

We have found that our clients fit into three general groupings: (1) those with a physical disability, (2) those who are disoriented, and (3) those who are experiencing a mental problem. Many of our people have long-standing behavioral problems that are aggravated by retirement, illness, death of a spouse, or lack of sufficient money. In addition, all these individuals are isolated from peers, medical resources, and other social and business institutions.

We serve approximately 120 participants on any one day; our active caseload is double that number. All participants, 40% of whom are in wheelchairs, are transported to the five neighborhood centers located throughout Tucson in vans equipped with hydraulic lifts.

Individuals who are most effective at serving clients are persons with the confidence to reflect upon their own emotional life and to accept themselves as they are. Many members of our program staff work exceptionally well with clients because they have achieved the depth of character that comes with living, making mistakes, and developing a good sense of humor about their own humanness. Reaching this point of maturity permits healthy introspection, and is close to being necessary to permit full concentration on the needs of others.

Reflection on our own emotional lives will show us that older people want what we want. They wish to be treated with respect—seemingly a lost art in this day and age. They wish to love and be loved. They wish to feel important, to feel appreciated, to make a difference to others. They wish to live in an environment they control, and one that contains extensions of their personalities. Finally, they want people to listen to them.

There is a tendency to overprotect the elderly which seems to originate in anticipating the guilt we might feel if something harmful happens to a person in our charge. Examples of this misguided concern are plentiful in any program that serves the frail and disabled elderly: overemphasis on strict adherence to a diet, restriction of physical activity, directed rest periods, worry about people getting over-excited. The normal risks of living are understood by older persons, who correctly view these risks as necessary to maintain a certain quality of life. The alternatives, though safer, are less interesting and certainly not stimulating.

Another important aspect of overprotection is denial of the right to make everyday decisions—small decisions about what to eat, what to do, where to sit. A disabled or disoriented elderly person evokes the parent in all of us. To deny anyone the opportunity to make small decisions creates dependency; at the same time it increases disengagement from the environment. For example, our clients often find it difficult to fill their leisure time at the Center; upon initial entry into the program, they quickly come to rely on staff to decide their activity for the day. It is hard not to answer the question, "What shall I do today?'' We know such decisions can be anxiety-producing: however, the anxiety and the process of solving such a problem exercises the mind and is beneficial to an individual's sense of self-reliance.

A person can be emotionally paralyzed at times, and in such a situation can be helped if provided limited choices: "You can read the book you started yesterday, or continue with your art work. Which do you prefer?" The person should not be permitted to escape into a world where everything is decided for him; this reduces the very coping skills that need to be kept active.

It should be remembered that a day care program which promotes maintenance of individuals in their homes philosophically accepts risks to mind and body as a necessary part of normal life. We allow our people to take reasonable risks in their fight to stay alive and involved.

Disabled and disoriented older people wish to be treated normally. To do otherwise is to become a part of their problem. They wish to be talked to in a normal tone of voice and to be expected to respond. They are interested in everyday subjects and activities. They want to be expected to accomplish tasks within their range of competency. Basically, they wish to contribute. To deny anyone this opportunity is to encourage psychological death.

The lunch served in a day care center is one of the main program activities. In our Center we try to use the family style meal as much as possible, and to have people take responsibility for some part of the meal process. It can get sloppy—people have received burns from hot coffee once or twice—but the total therapeutic effect is undeniable. Having a seriously disoriented person pass the napkins or set the table may be a slow process, but it is a healthy one.

Senior Health Improvement Programs has always served a large number of disoriented people and their families. Relatives of this particular group, trying to accomplish the difficult task of caring for the disoriented person, are starved for information that will help them provide more effective care. The respite provided them by day care makes their task possible. Staff has always felt a strong commitment to these people and enjoyment in developing innovative ways of keeping a disoriented person involved.

Touch is very important to this group, and holding the hand while conversing appears to aid concentration. The helper must be prepared to spend some time obtaining the desired verbal response. At first there may be no response at all, but verbal and facial activity increases as the contact continues. It is absolutely necessary to develop a degree of skill which will permit acceptance of the person "where he is." The content of a conversation initially may be quite bizarre, but the response must be in a normal tone of voice. Let me give you an example:

> "Arthur will be visiting me today," comes from a lady whose husband Arthur has been dead for ten years. There are some misguided helpers around who term it "reality therapy" to respond, "You know Arthur has been dead for ten years." These folks have no soul. This lady's memories of her husband may be so strong that Arthur *will* be visiting her today! Let's not quibble about the form the visitation will take. So I say, "Arthur is going to visit?" Response: "Yes. He always visits me and brings me flowers. Arthur is the kindest man." Helper: "Arthur must really care for you." Response: "Yes, he does. We love each other a great deal."

At this point you may have a good reason to add an element of reality to the conversation, and may reply, "You must miss him very much." However, the lesson to be remembered is this: talk to the person about the subject and feelings they wish to talk about. It can be uncomfortable to discuss covered wagons, chickens, and crossing creeks, as I have done; but if you can do so without being patronizing, you can add immeasurably to that person's enjoyment and feeling of worth. To express the words means something to the speaker, and at the minimum the words establish the contact that takes place through conversation.

The elderly, even more than the rest of us, wish others to take the time to listen to them and learn about them. It is comforting to have people know about you—what you are like; what you have learned. Your value is increased in your own eyes if someone else manifestly wants to hear what you have to say. Elderly people enjoy sharing with others information they have accumulated in their lifetime. This philosophy or wisdom is their legacy to others, and a sense of completeness is derived from successfully passing this legacy on to another obviously appreciative person. Listening and appreciating are two of our most effective tools.

This philosophical orientation is a buttress to the older person against some of the harsher realities that confront them. It should be recognized as a positive coping mechanism, and reflection on past experiences encouraged. Helpers in the program who enjoy hearing the philosophical conclusions of our participants are very successful in supporting this positive facet of their personalities and contribute a great deal to their happiness.

Each day care center has on staff a nurse who functions as a health counselor for the participant. With doctors as busy as they are, these nurses become very important to the health of our clientele. Available medical reports are often too brief or inaccurate. Each nurse has had to learn to rely on her skills of observation. The nurse has the opportunity to observe participants over a six-hour day and to experience the person totally; therefore, she becomes more expert than any other medical person about the status of each participant's health. Nurses collect information on fluids, aeration, nutrition, elimination, activity, pain. They counsel and educate the participant as to the things they can do at home and in the Center to maintain the highest level of health. Often they suggest a better diet, more activity, and/or less medication. The period of observation possible in the Center allows the nurse to observe symptoms not easily noted by the physician. Reporting these symptoms to the family physician results in a better diagnosis and better medical care.

The adult day care format of service provides our people wit! an environment in which the individual can function according to his own abilities. This environment provides a family of peers, physical care, education, leisure activities, and trips to many community events and places—all at a level that takes into account the intellectual and physical abilities of the participant. This society requires the individual to participate in making decisions and performing tasks. He or she must work out relationships with others, some of whom are at a high functional level, and others, lower. The members of the Center exert peer pressure on one another to accept the group's standards of behavior; in so doing, some degree of reactivation is forced in even the most withdrawn member. One participant will help another, perhaps by sharing some embarrassment felt when assisted to the bathroom or when helping another to the bathroom.

Families of participants are appreciated. They are respected for caring for mother or dad, since the Center staff knows what a task this is. Relatives and caretakers will become tired, angry, impatient, and at times rejecting. They are invited to Family Night at the Center in order to share with others their frustrations and to learn from others helpful information. If nursing home placement becomes unavoidable, we try to help the family understand why it is unavoidable and to ameliorate their feelings of guilt. the counseling that takes place is educational in nature, and hopefully provides the caretakers with information that makes their job easier. There is a strong mutual respect between staff and relatives that permits free exchange of information.

I hope that my admiration for the whole day care format is obvious. The positive elements inherent in the day care approach to delivering service never cease to excite this administrator.

A Training Program for Psychosocial Dimensions of Care in Long Term Care Facilities

14

Arthur N. Schwartz, Ph.D.

Psychosocial or mental health needs of elderly in long term care facilities deserve special attention. While the importance of factors which make life *possible*—physical care, medical services, public health components—is assumed, those elements of care which make life *worthwhile*—the psychosocial—have special significance for older persons.

In an effort to meet these psychosocial needs, a program has been developed to educate staff of long term care organizations. Such education should sensitize personnel and stimulate creative solutions. Improving the life space environment of an elderly person can compensate for losses and goes well beyond the "barrier-free environment" concept, as can be seen in the outline or guide which follows. The program has been designed (1) for in-service continuing education for long term care establishments and (2) as a model for teaching in other settings serving older persons.

The main objective should be made explicit to those participating: to teach staff people to learn to think, plan, and behave in ways that will help older residents maintain their own competence for living and sense of self-worth. An acceptable quality of life is not possible otherwise. To this end, the guide addresses important related issues in long term care:

1. Needs of staff persons themselves
2. Perceptions, needs, and involvement of family members.
3. Activity of people from outside the facility, such as volunteers and other community-based persons

The program is based on a model of training developed and tested in practice over a two-year period by the Andrus Gerontology Center, in collaboration with the California State Department of Health and funded by the National Institute of Mental Health. From that experience, strategies and procedures which achieved the above goals emerged.

Several general basic principles have emerged which apply to any effective in-service or continuing education enterprise:

1. Always prepare a class for a training series by developing positive expectations. This is accomplished by prior announcements that make clear when and where training will take place, who will participate, how much time will be spent, what is to be expected of students and of the instructor, what they can hope to get out of the training (job or career enhancement), and the like. Some of this should be done in advance of the class; some during the first session.

2. Make it clear that your training efforts are serious: your classes will take them only as seriously as you do. Non-verbal messages are probably much more important than verbal statements, announcements, or memos. Your trainees will begin to get the message that you place little importance on the training if the instructor is poorly prepared, for example, or not prepared at all; if the class is held in an inconvenient, unpleasant place subject to interruptions, disturbances, or constant annoyances; if classes are dropped even for good reasons or start very late consistently; if materials and equipment like adequate blackboards are lacking.

3. At the same time, to be successful you should see to it that the training is at the very least pleasant; at best, it can and should be intriguing, interesting, and even fun. There is no reason for such an enterprise to be grim, dull, or boring. Use references, visual aids, an

occasional interesting visiting lecturer or interview; employ role-playing, demonstrations, experience-sharing; offer refreshments or snacks; relax, be informal, use humor. Enjoy what can be for all a good experience.

4. Training should never be overly casual or abrupt. Ideally, no session should be less than 1 1/2 hours in length; 2 or 2 1/2 hours with perhaps a short 10 or 15 minute break is preferable. Continuity is also very important; better a 2 hour session or 1 1/2 hour session *every week* than 3 or 4 hours every second or third week or monthly. This program is geared to a 10 or 12 week series, which best facilitates the development of group cohesivenes. You will have gained an enormous advantage if you use the training to develop a sense of confidence and mutual trust in participants as well as to impart information. This will pay off in the short and long run. Also, do not use the class as a means of "getting at" your staff.

5. Be explicit, clear, and to the point. Sometimes a side issue is important to pursue, but you should keep the class on track or bring them back. You will want to draw discussion from your class, but make clear what you want, and the ultimate goals. Never let the class fall into petty bickering about a detail. If an issue is sticky, raise it in a concrete way and ask your class to brainstorm some creative solution.

6. Continuing education is to be seen as just that. *Everyone* on a long term care facility staff needs and deserves such an opportunity—even the night shift, office, and kitchen staff. They especially need such training. It should be repeated often enough to include all members of the staff.

7. Finally, some attention should be paid to evaluating the training. The trainer needs to know how effective the training is: where it is on target; where it needs improvement or revision. Effective evaluation requires setting very specific goals or objectives. At the very minimum you should ask for some evaluation during or at the end of the series. Three useful questions to ask for a *general* evaluation are:

a. What have you found most useful about this class?
b. What has interested you most?
c. What would you prefer to see changed—added, omitted, or given more time?

In this instance, some follow-up of improvements on the part of the staff or some survey of impact on the ultimate consumer, the resident (for which you might ask assistance), should prove revealing and helpful for further planning.

Design of Program

Each session in the original training series consisted of two basic parts. The first part was a morning seminar presentation and discussion on a central theme for the day, taking approximately 2 1/2 to 3 hours. The second part, conducted after lunch, consisted of a "Clinical Lab," a session of 2 hours or more of demonstration, interview, tape recording, film, etc., designed to amplify the morning's instructional theme.

These "clinical labs" can be incorporated into the presentation-discussion session. If the weekly sessions are limited to a 2-hour session, however, it would be wise to consider extending the length of the series (over a 14-16 week period) to allow ample time to explore adequately all the issues and problems raised.

Preliminary Planning Meeting
(Held about 2 weeks before classes begin)

Students for the original project were administrators and directors of nursing selected by State Department of Health Consultants who were familiar with the students and their locales. Teams of two from each of four (no more than six) facilities were selected.

For subsequent staff training purposes our experience indicated that approximately 8 to 16 persons make the optimal group size; these should be a mix from representative departments—housekeeping, food services, aides, R.N.'s, etc. An initial meeting with students in an informal setting for preliminary planning and orientation proved valuable.

Objectives

1. Introduce and get acquainted with instructors, participants, and consultants (if any), thus reducing any strangeness or discomfort.
2. Explain logistics and administrative details of the course, and answer the inevitable questions that people have.
3. Explain the general theme and goals of the course. Participants should have a pretty clear idea of where they are going in the course (goals) and how they'll get there.
4. Accomplish any pre-course evaluation.

Method:

1. Verbally share expectations, apprehensions, and reassurances encouraged by the trainer.
2. Discussion, questions, answers.
3. Have students draw themselves as they imagine themselves at about age 80 or 90; discuss attitudes toward aging suggested by drawings.
4. Give attitude-scale measure (attitudes toward the "old," or toward the job, or toward the facility); you can repeat this measure at the end and get some class help in interpretation if necessary.

This introductory session need not take over 1 hour, or 1½ hours at the most. It should create anticipation, arouse curiosity, and whet the learning appetite. At the same time, don't try to give the whole course at the first session.

Session 1

With Whom Are We Dealing?

I. Your attitude determines what you do.
   A. *How do you see* the residents or patients you care for?
      1. Your personal view of the old, the incapacitated: can you identify your own stereotypes, biases, and myths about old people?

2. The difference between being seen as persons *with* a disability and being seen as a disabled person.
3. What are the capacities, potentials, and "future" of the residents in your facility? (Write these on blackboards as they are verbalized by class. In other words, try to uncover your trainees' *expectations*.)

B. *Staff Coverage*
1. Who on the staff needs training?
2. How does one select staff? "x-y" theory: the view some hold that staff are not worth training (hired hands); another view: staff can be trained and can do more.
3. What does your staff need to know?
   a. *Your* answer and *their* answer (*ask* staff what need to know).
   b. Verbal and non-verbal messages (what you say vs. how you act).
   c. Training methods and procedures (spell out the procedures).
4. Talking mental health jargon to your staff—is jargon necessary to be understood? Or can we make ourselves understood better by reducing jargon (for example, using words like "walk" or "stroke" instead of "ambulate" or "CVA").

Important Points to Teach*

1. Learning can be fun, and enjoyable; in-service training should not be a bore.
2. Negative and positive attitudes toward aged residents generally held by staff persons and by older persons themselves should be explored; how this affects care.

*Note: Important points indicate how you might crystallize and sum up several important things you've gone over during the session so that participants leave the session with some clear idea of at least one, two, or three issues. This follows the old principle in education:
   1. Tell students what you are going to teach them.
   2. Teach them.
   3. Tell them what you have taught them.

3. Old people are constantly underestimated; they do have capacities, potentials, and futures. Discuss different expected goals for different persons.

References:

Schwartz, A. A transactional view of the aging process. In Schwartz, A., & Mensh, I. (Eds.). *Professional obligations and approaches to the aged.* Springfield, Ill.: Charles C. Thomas, 1974.

Shanck, A. Communication disorders: A problem in rehabilitation of the aged. In Burnside, I. (Ed.). *Psychosocial nursing care of the aged.* New York: McGraw-Hill, 1973.

Session 2

Objectives:

1. To become aware of some of the many possible events which may precede the admission of an elderly resident.
2. To understand the impact of the many losses that occur in the process of aging—physical losses, social losses, economic losses, loss of significant others, loss of role.
3. To show the importance of self-esteem in the total well-being of the aged person.
4. To encourage thinking along the lines of compensating for losses as the basic dimension of psychosocial (mental health) care.
5. To discourage the view of aging as an "incurable, irreversible disease."

Resident's "Career" Prior to Admission

I. Events in the resident's life which led up to admission.
   A. Many changes. Most represent losses; these losses, very gradual, usually cumulative, with many variations between individuals (not the same rate or extent).
      1. Physical changes: Energy, sight, hearing, taste, smell, touch, cardiovascular, "cosmetic", etc. Life is not the same at 80 as it was at 3. Give examples of various kinds of losses.

2. Social changes: Loss of family; friendship network is often disrupted through mobility, through death, sometimes through divorce.
3. Economic changes: Vocational and income loss, retirement, loss of home; many become poor when they retire, lose a friendship network upon retirement. Usually cannot compete in job market.
4. Cultural changes: Loss of significant, meaningful or desirable roles, often leads to "sick" role; agism —elderly are regularly de-valued, often assumed to be not as competent or useful as younger cohorts.

II. Psychological consequences of losses
  A. Relation of self-esteem, aging, and competence
    1. The rise and fall of self-esteem. Self-esteem grows out of positive feedback from others; is built on feeling of having impact on environment, or being an effective, competent person who "makes a difference," who counts.
    2. Functional model rather than chronic disease model. We sometimes spend so much time on pathology and deficits of aging we give old age a bad name.
  B. The notion of compensating for losses
    1. Example of things we attach to the body: eyeglasses, prosthetic legs, heart pacers, etc., are compensation devices.
    2. Don't penalize the old for their losses, don't make it harder for elderly to function (example—a nursery school must be designed to fit children, not penalize them).
    3. Going beyond "barrier-free environments": The environment must actually support function, make it easier to function physically, socially, emotionally, etc.

Important Points to Teach

1. Losses over the years need to be compensated so older persons can continue to function *in spite* of losses.
2. Self-esteem depends on a sense of competence and worthwhileness; this is critical to well-being and good health.

Reference:

Burnside, I. M. Loss: A constant theme in group work with the aged. *Hospital and Community Psychiatry,* 1970, *21*(6), 14-18.

Session 3

Objectives

1. List possible crises that precipitate admission.
2. Distinguish between a "gradually-developed" vs. a crisis decision.
3. Consider decision-making about admissions.
4. List important information needed on admission.
5. Define which types of admissions might be premature or unnecessary.
6. Explore available alternatives.

"Clinical Lab"

A. Role play:
  1. A guilt-ridden, angry family, seeking information about admission without the potential resident.
  2. A family accompanying the potential resident to admissions office.

  Role play from the *experiences* of participants. Explain that they are to play the roles from their memory of such persons' behaviors. Role play for a while, call a halt, and allow other participants to role play until all have had the experience. One person should play the administrator, the D.N., and/or admitting clerk; try combinations of these.
B. Have students draw themselves in old age in crisis situation which necessitates being sent to a nursing home. Discuss varieties of crisis and prevention.

Factors Precipitating Admission

I. A gradually-developed or a crisis decision?
  A. Whose decision? What kind of referral? What source?
    1. How was your facility selected?

      2. Appropriate selection; life-style factors (will life style of resident be facilitated or frustrated?)
- B. The family as a source of information
  1. What kind of "history" is important to know? Should you only be concerned about health history? What about family relationships, family processes?
  2. Direct and indirect means of:
     a. getting information
     b. giving information
     Look for tell-tale signs of strain between family members, tendency to "con" the potential resident; what information is obviously omitted?

II. Is this admission right?
- A. Premature or unnecessary admission
  Can the family really care for the relative? Will this do more harm than good; is this a "dumping" phenomenon?
- B. Are there real alternatives?
  1. Who makes the decision? Do you *tell* them, or explain the alternatives and their relative merits?
  2. Do you counsel or refer?
     Should you help the family, and if so, how?

Important Points to Teach

1. Gradual vs. crisis decision: different ways of handling.
2. Older person needs time and support to adjust to change.
3. Increase the supports by staff for all newly admitted persons.
4. Share information with one another so that staff responses are appropriate.

Session 4

Objectives

1. Explore and describe the attitudes and moods of residents upon admission.

2. Sensitize to the effects of first impressions both staff and new residents.
3. Develop new and better ways to orient the new resident, soften the transfer trauma, and help newcomers deal with a novel set of circumstances.

"Clinical Lab"

Show the film *Peege,* and discuss from point of view of family relationships.

The Resident at Time of Admission

I. How does the resident view the move into a facility?
   A. What has he been told or not told about the move? What about the resident who has been "conned" or misled; what about resultant "confusion"?
   B. What are resident's biases, expectation, attitudes?
      1. Toward the family. Good or poor family history? Is the resident angry at members of family (does resident exploit this, through guilt)?
      2. Toward the facility? Write on blackboard the biases verbalized by staff; how to deal with negative ones.
   C. What about the first impression of the resident?
      Give examples from own experience how first impressions work—good and bad; first impressions of seeing something unpleasant through an open door—how can this affect the new person?
II. Orienting the new resident
   Need to see the whole facility from an upright, not horizontal position. Review losses of the older person; in addition to problems with vision, hearing, etc., now in a new, strange place.
   A. Purpose of introduction, use of first names
      People are very important (roommates). Who does what? Whom does one go to? What can the new resident expect?
   B. Thorough familiarization (need to repeat)
      Don't assume a single introduction or tour is sufficient. Options: daytime tour, night-time tour; use of a picture, a map, a "buddy"; residents as hosts or hostesses.